OCCULT PHILOSOPHY

FOR THE MODERN AGE

Mysticism
Metaphysics
Theoretical Science
Philosophy

Written and Illustrated by Tarl Warwick
2015

OCCULT PHILOSOPHY

Neither this work nor any part thereof may be replicated, distributed, sold, or altered without the express written consent of the author.

OCCULT PHILOSOPHY

INTRODUCTION

Within the occult, as within any other field of study, it is important to note correlation and correspondence between systems. In the west, we regard time as linear, and fields of study (often) as divorced from one another. Here, I will refute this and cover a wide spectrum of occult topics, from history, to science as yet not fully understood, to mathematics and spirituality itself (for the spiritual is merely one component of the occult.)

I seek here to illuminate the reader; for our human understanding of the world, while growing, is as yet dim and limited- to compare the light of man's current knowledge with the light it will shine in a thousand years is like comparing a half-dead flickering light bulb to the sun itself. There is no comparison, and understanding must continuously grow.

All theories, all beliefs, all spiritual tenets, must be exposed for public review, for it is a fact of the capability to progress that ideas will become purified over time; they will compete, and that which does not fit during an era will be destroyed, only to be revived later on when it is necessary for it to be so- when the ethos behind it is more appropriate and fitting. Here in this work, I will dwell upon philosophy and show finally to the world my own findings as they currently stand.

Within the occult there are thousands of schools- so often even open minded occultists will join one of these paths and exclude themselves from even studying the others. So, too, may the practitioner regretfully expel science and logic from their study and experimentation and dwell instead in the antiquated (and unrealistic) belief that only pure spirituality with no secular basis is "true" or "real" occultism. Here I must remind all; the occult is both the common basis for secular study, as well as its compatriot. Not all occult texts deal with folk spells, hexes, and demons, and it would be dishonest to claim that they are. Purists and skeptics alike will balk at the inclusion of the spiritual and secular together, often without regarding the actual history of occult philosophy.

OCCULT PHILOSOPHY

We will see here that all things move together- there are definite connections in all fields of human endeavor, and with nature- the two are essentially the same. We often say man is artificial, man's creations are artificial- this is true, in a subjective sense, yet man is *a part* of nature and inescapably so. We are animals, at our core, and although we may attempt to rise steadily above this and become something more, we remain organic life forms bound to certain physical laws- physical laws which are malleable because the way in which we interpret reality changes over time. This will form one of the major bases upon which this work is built.

Likewise, we must regard a long span of human history, and in doing so we can see, for certain; culture, philosophy, spirituality, and all other realms of understanding affect one another, are affected by the others, and by nature as well. There are philosophical components here to be derived purely from observing this natural state of the world- there are lessons to be learned, which some will take to heart and others reject. So be it.

Behind much of this is the concept *as above so below*. Mostly, this is applied to the world in such a way as to read instead "the spiritual world must be a reflection of the physical world, so we understand the former through the latter." This oversimplification also works in reverse, for thus the physical world is also a reflection of the spiritual. We see the world as a negative- we hold it up to the light and see only a reflection of reality- one incorporating all of our bias and all of our anthropic beliefs. These are perfectly fine for understanding the subjective aspects of reality- for academic studies for academic purposes. What, though, does it benefit us in terms of the actually spiritual? It has no benefit- because any understanding we derive will also be subjective only.

This is however not a bad thing- for I will make the claim that the most fringe, spectacular, subjective, and even unlikely beliefs are theoretically true- everything that can be imagined is real in some other dimensional plane, and merely observing the world around us we will see that things move in patterns.

OCCULT PHILOSOPHY

I do not mean to say that I believe in determinism- quite the opposite, I refute it on the basis that I don't see the cosmos as finite and a closed system, but rather an infinite and open one, but within this cosmos are smaller systems which indeed are *mostly* closed, at least for very long periods of time as we conceive of it. In this sense, we can regard cycles, subjectively, as interlocking, affecting one another, and affecting even the way we view the world. Even celestial movements, mostly fixed for long periods as they are, affect our world- astronomy being of course one of the earliest fixtures of both secular and occult study.

Mathematics matters- so too does history. And philosophy above all, at least insofar as it informs our understanding and governs our emotional response to the things we encounter in life.

I do not offer this work as an objective guide to life, or as a compilation of what you may think I regard as objectively true fact set in stone for all the ages, but rather as a guide to understanding the occult manner of the way things *appear* to be, or are, but for merely a time. We could exist for a million years and it would be a mere blink of the eye in the life of the cosmos, and it is with this in mind that I expose the content here for others to absorb.

There are many occult truths to be covered here. The nature of reality, the interconnected web of physical and spiritual cycles which govern not just the occult but all of mans endeavors, and the importance of psychotropics as well as other topics, among other things. It is through these cycles, and the struggles they create, that man is purified spiritually as well as physically.

OCCULT PHILOSOPHY

TABLE OF CONTENTS

THE PHILOSOPHY OF INTERCONNECTED TIME
-
THE MANNER OF THE DIMENSIONS
-
FINITE PARTS, INFINITE SYSTEM
-
THE MOON CYCLE
-
THE SUN CYCLE
-
THE IMPORTANCE OF DIVINE NUMBERS
-
THE PLANETS
-
THE CYCLE OF THE MAN
-
THE CYCLE OF THE SEASONS
-
THE CYCLE OF THE AGES
-
THE CYCLE OF PHILOSOPHY
-
THE CYCLE OF CULTURE
-
THE CYCLE OF SPIRITUALITY
-
EVOLUTION OF NON-BIOLOGICAL PRINCIPLES

TABLE OF CONTENTS (cont.)

EASTERN PHILOSOPHY IS WRONG

-

WESTERN PHILOSOPHY IS WRONG

-

NOTHING ENDS: MORALITY IS SUBJECTIVE

-

ORDER FROM CHAOS

-

INTERCHANGEABILITY OF MATTER

-

PSYCHOTROPICS AS PENULTIMATE

-

THE DIVINE ENDEAVORS

-

ONE GOD MANY FORMS: ONE LIFE MANY FORMS

-

FREEDOM IS THE HIGHEST TRUTH

-

CARE FOR NATURE REFLECTS CARE FOR US

-

DEATH IS AN ILLUSION

-

VIBRATION: DIMENSIONS AS RADIO STATIONS

-

BEYOND THE VEIL OF DEATH

-

CONCLUSION

OCCULT PHILOSOPHY

THE PHILOSOPHY OF INTERCONNECTED TIME

The human animal has for so long observed that the world around him is connected to the procession of time; it does not matter, whether he regards it as a line, or a circle, or as a spiral in which things sometimes repeat, or as a branch whereby his free will determines the twig upon which he will grow the bulk of the tree of life.

All of these systems are woefully mistaken, for each one looks at just one measure of time, excluding all others- this is akin to a person looking at a beautiful painting through a single lens, such that he can only observe one small piece at a time. Gather together ten people in such an arrangement, and they will all look at different parts of the painting, and derive different conclusions to its form and meaning, without any of them seeing the whole for what it really is. "It is a nose" says one of them, observing the nose of a figure painted there. "No, it is a field of flowers" says another, seeing only part of the foreground. Another may see a tree, or the moon, or anything else painted thereupon, but unless they remove their filtered lenses, which inform their view of reality, none of them will ever see the entire truth.

With this in mind we observe the spiritual man, who operates in much the same manner. The way a human lives, the decisions they make, everything that they believe themselves to "know" is entirely informed by the very small amount that they actually observe in the world- not a single one of them sees it all. The physical man would be unable, in his short life, to observe the entire planet Earth, let alone the cosmos, and thus in his physical state it is not possible for him to understand all physical truth. Even insofar as science and philosophy have illuminated the world, they are merely dull rays illuminating a very small portion of observable reality.

OCCULT PHILOSOPHY

How much more, then, is the spiritual world dark, when all of the religions and spiritual philosophies regard the others as horrible, heretical, and evil? Each person is compelled, by these monstrous religious orders, to believe in only one piece of reality; each one is told what to observe, how to interpret it, and what to ignore. The spiritual world, in a way, is darker and less illuminated than even the blackest cave in which shines only a single candle.

In this condition most people in the world are scarcely able to remark on the spiritual, since the spiritual that they observe is so minute in nature; and even when these filters are removed from them and they begin to see more, so often they bring their own former bias with them and unconsciously continue to base reality on their own assumptions.

Understanding the deep and interconnected cycles and levels of creation is paramount in then understanding ourselves for the physical is mirrored with the spiritual; it is through understanding these concepts that the occultist and the scientist become the same thing; for in our modern era, and in times past, the two have remained separate, and ages of expansion and progress most often coincide with eras in which the two showed less hostility towards one another. We look around us, and see the great cities and roads and vehicles and airplanes and weapons and medicine, and we say science has created such things, and that religion has held them all back as well as it could; this is half true, for organized religion is the exclusion (mostly) of science just as doctrinal science in its secular manner is the exclusion of all spirituality. Here I have to say; spirituality and religion are *not* the same thing; and the latter denies science altogether wherever science challenges its doctrine, while the former embraces science, at least insofar as it is credible, notwithstanding that some "science" is forcibly injected for political reasons and has little validity.

OCCULT PHILOSOPHY

There is much material to cover here that the human race must understand; the grand design of the cosmos must be revealed at last, although it is impossible for any finite being to fully comprehend and document it; we can do our best though at trying, and certainly when the veils of the finite are removed it is possible to begin comprehending the infinite.

We first must ask ourselves simply "is there a limit to time and space?" I say to this unequivocally, "No." This seems obvious; for if we consider the observable universe we can perhaps theorize that it is surrounded by a brick wall or some other crude representation for a cosmic barrier, but upon considering what is on the other side, it must be habitable space even if it is empty beyond the edges of the universe and stretches, empty, for infinity on all "sides." It is able, however, to be inhabited by matter and energy regardless of how empty it may seem. Perhaps it's not even empty at all and we're in a false vacuum.

I do not fear science; neither does any actual occultist- those claiming to be spiritual while saying science is useless are hedonist throwbacks to the grosser elements of paganism which simultaneously ignore pagan philosophy and pagan medicine and pagan technological advances. Before anybody reading these words should assume that I thus would desire a world of steel and cement without nature I should say that is not my intent; but the cosmos themselves are ordered, and *must* be ordered simply because order arises spontaneously and instantly wherever an existence has been spawned. And these existences are infinite too in number, yet paradoxically *do not exist at all* except as arbitrary placeholders when thought about from a dimension higher than their own.

This material is dense, it is difficult for man to comprehend; but if one wishes to truly master the occult, it *must* be comprehended. For this reason I say to those who practice genuine magick; science is not to be denied nor feared, but rather embraced and studied with great critical thinking and rationality.

OCCULT PHILOSOPHY

VIVIVI

VIVIVI

VIVIVI

VIVIVI

OCCULT PHILOSOPHY

THE MANNER OF THE DIMENSIONS: DIVINE MATHEMATICS

The first thing that must be cast aside is man's tendency to either not comprehend or to misconstrue the nature of what infinity means, from a mathematical perspective.

If you ask a person what infinity means they will be unable to actually denote it; because everything they observe is finite, but there is a relatively simple mathematical answer for the infinite, and the way to properly represent it is so simplistic as to seem almost foolish to some; the infinite is represented purely as the number "1."

The reader will now balk at this early stage of this work; how can a finite number represent an infinity? I say, it does; because "1" merely represents a singular, expanse-less whole. The finite mathematical systems we make use of are just infinitely small decimals derived from that same number, with nonexistence (or any lower dimension) represented by the number "0."

I will here depict the nature of the dimensions, and their repeating form, which is arbitrary for the most part but represents the best possible image we can make to explain it, at least from our own perspective; for here perspective matters:

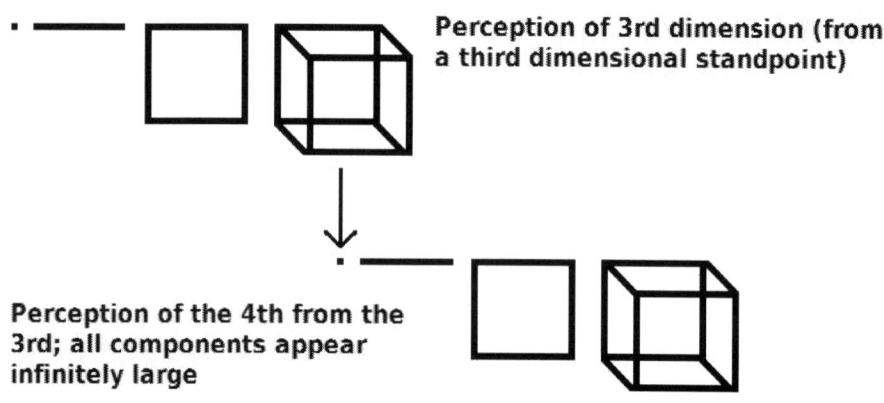

OCCULT PHILOSOPHY

Any dimension when observed or conceived of from a higher dimension merely contains the ultimate value of zero- it must, for it doesn't exist on the higher dimension except as a placeholder with no actual tangible form. We, for example, represent the second dimension as a sheet; but really since it has no depth it does not exist at all when perceived of from our own dimension. This is the same when ours is regarded from the fourth.

Any dimension witnessed from the one below it carries the value of "1" representing that it composes an infinite compilation of numbers of the lower. It would take an infinite number of third dimensions to comprise one fourth dimensional plane; for each third dimension is infinitely small compared to it. If a being on the fourth dimension were able to see our dimension they would see it as a series of snapshots in time and would consider us as limited as we would consider a being in the second dimension able to move up, down, forwards and back, but not to the side.

In our own dimension as represented by those within it we attempt to allot it the value of infinity but all of our mathematics cannot fill this goal; a number, regardless of how large, will never actually reach that "1" which comprises it- our finite mathematical systems merely deal with decimals between zero and one. This is a mathematical paradox; zero times infinity when expressed equates to an undefined number because it is not possible to ever finish the multiplication involved (because the number of multiplications is infinite.) I use here the number "1" as yet another arbitrary placeholder only because it represents the singular whole, undivided.

Within the previous picture, each minute point merely represents an infinitely long decimal approaching zero in value *from the perspective of one within the dimension itself.* A detached observer would likely see no difference between any values at all and they would merely become part of some strange cosmic totality.

OCCULT PHILOSOPHY

Herein we see the basis for the reincarnation process- a three dimensional being may die and be destroyed on this dimension, however their termination point physically overlaps with the birth of another at some point along this line, and in the fourth dimension the fact that their consciousness has been destroyed is meaningless- only the fact that we are dimly at best aware of the upper dimension prevents us from realizing that the same *ego* we possess here is at work elsewhere; the self has been split up, for what reason none knows but many surmise. Perhaps, as some claim, this was conscious and decided, and "we" decided to partition ourselves so as to experience a number of lives as a finite being, for the sole purpose of our own amusement. Perhaps, likewise, we are all really the same being expressing itself in an infinite number of ways for eternity.

There are of course other theories as to how the dimensions are arranged- most take up an egocentric assumption that our own is unique and that our observable physical laws and mathematical systems are special somehow; which seems unlikely if we truly are merely one of a number of observable planes. If there are other dimensions, it seems sensible to say that perhaps our understanding is even more dim than most believe, for these laws may not be at work on those above or below; here we get oddly enough the occult statement "as above so below"- upon applying this logic to reality itself a repeating mechanized system such as that which I here theorize begins to make more sense, although similar designs could also be feasible and plausible.

Some believe that there are ten dimensions; I ask why we should presume that there are only ten, and have not yet received a satisfactory explanation; perhaps it is limited to these ten because beyond that lies some sort of bizarre realm which we are unable to even theoretically comprehend.

OCCULT PHILOSOPHY

FINITE PARTS, INFINITE SYSTEM

Here we must express another cycle and another mathematical concept which is at work in our existence which is of occult importance; that of randomization.

If we presume that the observable universe (by which I mean not readily observed, but rather able to be observed) is infinite in dimensions, then it can be subject to truly random processes. If, instead, it is finite, randomization without a cosmic backing would be an illusion, but ultimately this matters little, because the convolution of reality is so great as to approach the random. I will explain this further but will preface it with my opinion that the third dimension is infinite in scope because there is no process by which it may be limited- in essence, even if we posit a field of energy at its "edges" preventing matter from inhabiting the other side, there is still some plane or existence beyond this invisible, theoretical barrier. Here I will state a series of assumptions.

First, that if the third dimension is limitless and there is no cosmic, intelligent force behind its creation, then the universe, however it was spawned, is not unique and that in this limitless expanse, whatever random process created our own universe has almost surely spawned others.

Second, if it is limitless and there *is* an intelligent cosmic force behind it, this cosmic force or being could have spawned other such universes anyways. In this limitless expanse, whether willed by a creator or created by random and not yet understood processes, it seems almost impossible that there is no other intelligent life other than man (by mathematical virtue alone, assuming our planet inhabits a place somewhere in the middle of a bell curve on the subject of size, composition, and so forth)- but this issue is peripheral and merely interesting.

OCCULT PHILOSOPHY

Third, if the expanse of our reality is limited, we have to determine the nature of the matrix beyond its borders and prescribe some explanation as to how it is limited to begin with; while I feel this is unlikely, I have to assume that if true it deals with curving space-time, and perhaps the edge is represented as the location where our reality merges with some other dimension.

As systems become more convoluted they approach randomization. It is not possible, truly, to know if such a system is infinite (and random) or finite but convoluted (and thus deterministic without being obviously so.)

We can detail this easily. Envision as it were a machine which contains only two gears working in tandem, with a digital display which reads their respective counts. This machine is orderly, mechanized, and easily understood- it has only two interconnected moving parts, and none would say that it operates on any random principle.

Now envision a machine with a billion such interconnected readings, each influencing the operations of the other- perhaps one causes the sum of all others to divide by some arcane and arbitrary total- another to multiply it. One gear when activated at certain points cancels several others out. Another reverses the digits. A billion counts each influencing the others on the basis of their own mechanical and orderly processes, and their own mechanical and orderly natures, yet in this situation the machine's display will seem to spit out more or less random numbers forever; in time, with an enormous amount of study and experimentation, its full function is *technically* able to be quantified such that it would be possible to accurately predict each reading in turn, but the effort would be gargantuan and the time needed quite long; as such any individual looking at its readings would declare it to be a random generation of numbers within whatever defined limits have been given.

OCCULT PHILOSOPHY

With this in mind, it is perhaps not possible to know whether we live in a deterministic reality, or one which is truly random, because it would require an inordinate amount of observation and experimentation to determine the nature thereof. If, as I believe, the universe we reside in is merely one of an infinite number, we might say it is *technically impossible* to decide which is the case- a paradox because a universe with limited edges residing in endless emptiness and solitude will, to us, appear identical to one residing in a largely empty matrix of third dimensional space, which nonetheless holds other universes so far away from our own that the chance of one coming close enough to be witnessed is at best negligible and quite likely altogether near impossible.

It does not, however, even truly matter which is the case- a nearly limitless mechanized arrangement will at least *appear* to be random. In either case, the universe, assuming it is divorced from any others that might exist by the vastness of the near-vacuum of space, operates like its own separate gigantic mechanism. The planets, stars, lunar bodies, asteroids and comets, star dust and debris, even man-made objects, all move in tandem in a fashion not unlike that of a gigantic and convoluted clock- this spawns the basis for the watchmaker god, the deist argument that a cosmic creator invented reality and then sat back to watch it with relative passivity, observing it out of boredom or curiosity- whether such a creator is loving, hateful, or neutral depends on whether we imagine the small boy watching a tank of fish decides to feed them, or watch them starve to death out of malicious delight.

Truly speaking the universe is one of a number- it would be an oversimplification to state that the number is infinite because the universes are almost surely arranged in a manner not unlike that which we observe in atoms- and perhaps the universe is less like an atom and more like a quark. In this limitless cosmos where the value of all energy and matter approaches 1, anything and everything is real, at the same time; all deities, somewhere, reside- Asgard is indeed real, as is Hell, and humans have a part in creating these things because on lower dimensions each concept we create mentally exists as its own infinite existence. Guard thy thoughts.

OCCULT PHILOSOPHY

THE MOON CYCLE

The lunar cycle here pertains to the occult in the most penultimate manner; there is a reason why this work regards it as more intrinsic to biology than the solar cycle, for it is a better indicator of almost all cycles.

Let us consider the woman's period- for it is a lunar measurement involved; its average measure is roughly the same length as one lunar cycle, give or take a week or so- if we attempt to measure this on solar terms we are left with ourselves attempting to approximate it to one month, but the twelve months themselves are concerned mostly with seasons and with the weather where this calendar system was first used in major form; essentially the upper Mediterranean; the twelve months as they exist make little sense in a tropical climate, where wet and dry seasons are of greater importance than cold and warm seasons, and it would make less sense, say, in the cold and frozen far north, where there may be six months of freezing temperatures and two months of total warm weather. Regardless of the zone, though, the human body retains more or less its homeostasis and the lunar, not solar cycle, determines the period.

Likewise the period in which a human is formed in the womb- nine months yes, but also nine lunar cycles; for the month here is also peripheral, although it is a close approximate. It is the moon which matters- and it is indeed the nocturnal which matters also given the manner in which the human was conceived to begin with; likely at night with curtains drawn and the full action of left hand path lust at work.

Most biological systems relate more closely to the lunar than the solar- how odd it is then that the lunar in new age mythology is sworn to the spiritual and the solar to the physical; perhaps this overlooks a very much higher truth; that the solar and lunar cycles *both* reign over physicality and spirituality- merely that they are waning when the physical comes into force and waxing when the spiritual does so.

OCCULT PHILOSOPHY

Here we regard the nature of ritualism and ceremony; Easter being of course a combined rite- it takes place with regards both to the solar and lunar, being dated according to the equinox (a solar event) and the moon cycle subsequent to it. This fertility rite is that which ends all others; and was practiced in the pagan era with various orgiastic rites and drunkenness. Even the christianized version practiced in the west today retains the same solar and lunar element, and all the trappings of a sex ritual are there also, for eggs and rabbits are conspicuous in their more authentic use.

It is strange that so many agricultural species, from seed to maturity, achieve their final form in 60 or 90 or 120 days- purely lunar measurements which have little to do with the same sun which shines upon them and causes them to grow. This strangeness begins to dissipate when we regard the claim that it isn't sun that primarily influences human mood (or the growth of other life forms) but rather the lack thereof- the dark period, the nocturnal- the time at which the pineal gland is not being bombarded with cosmic rays and begins to exude its influence, the time in which the plant is not growing and is temporarily in stasis.

Here we have another consideration; we must now determine whether biological life forms are unique or interchangeable. A sterile, purely secular view would claim that life forms are not special and arose largely through mathematical chance; a similar situation to that in which order spontaneously arises from chaos only because the mathematical odds of this approach 1- if this is so, so be it. Spiritual individuals have the odd habit of reacting badly to this claim of mechanized existence without realizing that if it is true, it actually gives evidence to the claim of reincarnation (literally, because the ego is thus also not unique and, like any other mechanized system, can be retained, even if the person's ego leaves the body while doing so, forgetting its past third dimensional existence!)

OCCULT PHILOSOPHY

Likewise, if these biological systems *are* unique, then we have to speak of the nature of its cause- if they are unique, special, not interchangeable, then surely there is some purpose to them, because they would need to have been designed by some intelligence or other cosmic phenomenon. Again, so be it; this again preserves the ego upon death because the ego is unique and almost surely created by some divine hand; which hand created it matters little, for man's conceptions of afterlives, hells, heavens, paradise and purgatory, are all easily explained within the dimensional structure; a hell is just the result of creating a thought-form about such a place and then digressing into the second dimension upon physical death, with heaven being the same, only with a different thought form; it would seemingly last for an eternity because it was composed on a higher dimension. (Here I use the term "second dimension" not to mean a flat plane, for a being within it would experience it the same way we experience the third- the being would have a depth which comprises a decimal partition of the whole, which is only infinitely small ("0") from our perspective, not from that of such a being.)

At the same time, a paradise could also be created which is even more blissful- the fourth dimension would be a lot like the astral realm predicted by the Theosophists and other groups. Within this divine mathematical system perhaps we must regard the limitations as not *infinite* but *near infinite*. It is unthinkable that if there is a divine being, that this being would will creations which are finite to infinite punishment for some minor transgression they were often not aware they were committing.

Likewise if the ego is not unique then much like the lunar or solar cycles, any existence will pass, even if it appears to take "forever" for it to do so. In this manner an ego must experience limitless lives.

The new age regards the lunar as spiritual and gives the supposed cult behind it the name *Luminari*. They oppose this with the Illuminati, and envision these prelates as inhabiting a subterranean world called *Agartha*.

OCCULT PHILOSOPHY

How very strange that the lunar people would be subterranean given the connection between lack of light (the night or sleep cycle) with psychic abilities, dreams, visions, and the spiritual world of the light-sensitive pineal gland. Conspiracies aside, one must wonder if there is more here than is being said, for this is regarded by some as fringe truth and by some as fringe nonsense.

The lunar cycle however truly reigns over the physical more than the spiritual in many ways; at least insofar as its very absence is important within these biological systems *as they relate to the spiritual!* Attempting to disconnect these two is folly; in reality the spiritual is a manifestation of the physical mind and the physical is a reflection of the spiritual world intertwined with it, neither can exist without the other being present. If we observe early man we see he had a fondness for psychotropics and music and had some sort of burial rites in full effect several tens of thousands of years ago in Neanderthal culture (and I say culture because that is what it indeed was; they were not brutes, but rather sophisticated.)

The absence or near absence of light is important; the lunar reigns over this cycle, but can only evoke the spiritual as long as there is a physical realm for it to act upon; here is where every spiritual school has failed, for they categorize the spiritual and physical as separate forces, opposing forces, almost like the two poles of a magnet, but they are inconsequential and indeed nonexistent without one another. This is the very basis for magick. The left hand and right hand paths have fought for thousands of years, each without realizing it is in combining these two schools that true magick and true spirituality occurs- it is not possible for a person to ever truly leave their physical existence, at least not permanently, nor can a physical form expect to forever be bereft of spirituality. The same way a child is born from a male and female force combining, equates to the spiritual world; for when the physical and spiritual approximate one another, there is wisdom, finally.

OCCULT PHILOSOPHY

We see another conclusion from this rumination; The lunar and solar cycles must also be considered in relation to one another, not as separate or opposing forces, *per se*.

They are technically opposing forces on an anthropomorphic level; man has decided to split them apart because man's understanding of the world often relies upon noting opposing forces even if they are not opposed. We say, the sun is lord of the day and the moon lords over the night, but both are visible celestial bodies, and both shine light (the moon of course does not make its own and merely reflects light)- even with this there is more similarity than difference, because it indicates that the same light comes from both bodies, one is merely reflecting it and the other directly producing it.

Thus these two forces, considered at odds by the untrained, are actually similar more than they are separate; here the occult appears to have overlooked this and split into groups which primarily regard lunar cycles and complicated lunar ephemera, and those which consider solar holidays or eclipses more important. These eclipses, considered of such vast intrigue by so many cultures both past and present, are in fact also the result of the solar and lunar forces interacting; whether it be a blood moon or a situation in which the moon, for a moment, comes between sun and Earth and appears to blot the former out from our view.

The moon is additionally important however; as the herald of the left or sinister path, the feminine force. Here we must draw a fairly complicated correlation however. The sun is a masculine force- it creates its own power and the feminine reflects this male power, however it is the *female* lunar power most connected to the same physical cycles despite being just a reflection of the male spiritual and physical force. The solar, reigning over the day, shines down infinite energy to the planet, yet it is distant when compared to the feminine; the moon is physically closer, controlling the tidal cycles as well, which much like any other ecological cyclical system renew and refresh the coastal regions, cleaning detritus and depositing it for feeding. It provides all life.

OCCULT PHILOSOPHY

Nobody has ever claimed that the sun would drive them mad but they have made that claim indeed about the moon. Perhaps in these Renaissance era tales we are seeing not objective reality but rather their opinion because they were lorded over by solar kings and abrahamic philosophy; nonetheless the sacred feminine of the left hand path appears to have made the same mistake in elevating the female without regard, specifically, to the presence of a dominant male force as well.

We might call this philosophy the twain path, or the connected path, or something along these lines- regarding neither the lunar nor solar as intrinsically more important but merely regarding them as connected cycles.

Here I will reveal another truth- over the great distance of time all cycles coincide eventually; the length required to be observed to see them all overlap at the right moment is astronomically high- perhaps billions of years- but there would, we expect, through either random process or divine will, at some future date, come a point at which the moon is at the exact moment of fullness right as the solstice punctuates with a lunar eclipse, right as a major extinction occurs. This statement seems unreasonable and strange, but has a purpose I assure you; for it shows that even in a randomized infinite existence, if time is infinite so is the eventual chance that all of these cycles will coincide.

It is sad, watching so many people in this world think about it only in terms of opposing forces; while this is how man primarily understands physical reality, it does little to understand the spiritual other than conflate its nature with the physical- I have stated that the two correspond and this is true, but *the nature we observe is merely subjective and not objective.* We are finite, and the ability we have to truly observe the nature of the cosmos is finite as well. We can only begin understanding the true spiritual nature of reality by forsaking the concept of opposing forces and instead drawing comparisons between forces and phenomenon we once described as "opposites." The lunar and solar are a major feature of this fact.

OCCULT PHILOSOPHY

OCCULT PHILOSOPHY

THE SUN CYCLE

The solar cycle actually has more to do with the occult in a spiritual sense in some ways than the lunar cycle does- let us reckon the average lifespan that seemingly was enjoyed by man before the age of modern medicine; in all cases in any developed region by the bronze age the average lifespan for those who survived infancy seems to have been about sixty years (burial remains show a freakishly high infant mortality rate, but those surviving the first few years typically did quite well.) There are twelve months in the calendar and this lifespan is five times twelve years, or thereabouts- and while our mathematical system is arbitrary, the arrangements and diminutions given in the measure of time frequently rely upon biological principles; which makes sense, since the celestial and biological cycles coincide.

The sun itself rotates- this was not known long ago, although the movement of sunspots across its surface was already noted in the Renaissance. The sun rotates every roughly 24 days- twelve times two. There seem to be quite a few 12's in the solar.

The sun reigns over the masculine force, and it is indeed a powerful object; were it not for this gigantic (and still partly enigmatic) ball of fiery plasma shining in the center of our solar system there would be no life on this planet, except perhaps chemotrophic, subterranean life forms able to gain energy from volcanic systems influenced by the moon more than the sun. From time to time the sun fires out waves of energy in various directions- the Carrington Event in the 1800s destroyed telegraphic systems and caused numerous problems on the planet, and was caused by a large solar flare; the result of such a flare today would be the decimation of most electronics on the earth's surface including most power plants and power lines, which would short out, causing explosions and fires and probably killing millions as firestorms erupt in urban locales. The sun is a giver of life but it can take it as well; as anyone familiar with melanoma understands.

OCCULT PHILOSOPHY

How odd that the masculine force here represents physicality even though the female is the one gestating the infant- still stranger that the sun is identified as the giver of life when the moon perturbs the world and stirs the core, keeping it molten. Were humans an aquatic species, we might regard the moon and the feminine force as the physical force and the sun above, permeating only a few yards into the water, as of spiritual importance- especially since it would require ascension to the air above to fully feel its effects.

The solstices and equinoxes are of course the most important events with regards to the solar, within the realm of the occult, and it would be strange not to regard them considering their important mathematical function as well as their reign over the physical seasons. The sun is a potent energetic force, and the primary one which gives life directly to the planet. Agriculture is impossible without it, even though it is also capable of degrading things over the slow course of the ages through its penultimate release of photons.

In artistic imagery within solar religions such as christianity we often see allusions to the dominant male potency of the sun- observe any Renaissance-era depiction of their messiah, and you will note the presence of a halo over his head which is quite literally the light of their god. This is a solar symbol- for it is the sun of god, behind the son of god, within their pantheon- a metaphor and symbol of their savior as the giver of redemption just as the sun is the giver of life within the same belief system. Within other artistic renderings we see the same. Muhammad is depicted with the same solar energies, although depictions of this prophetic figure are more often associated with flame than with the sun, and depict him almost burning with an aural flame surrounding his body, although you will see the same solar halo applied as well from time to time. Perhaps here we are seeing the deliberate omission of the latter by some artists who felt it heretical and believed that the energetic possession was to be depicted, but that the light, even for their prophet, was a separate force, while Jesus, said to be god's son, was able to wield it directly.

OCCULT PHILOSOPHY

We see solar imagery elsewhere as well; light is everywhere, and its use within the artistic does not necessarily even connect to the divine, for its imagery is also within the blatantly fictional. We get here the idea of a film in which the forces of evil are (almost invariably) represented by darkness and a sudden blinding light either cripples or burns them, such as the popular image of the wizard Gandalf as wielding, in Tolkein's own quasi-mythology, the *Flame of Anor* which some consider to be a direct representation of the sun. Some of his fictional exploits closely mimic those found with Jesus in the bible.

However we must now consider something again in terms of this non-dichotomy I have spoken of, for light and darkness are not opposing forces so much as complimentary ones. Let us imagine ourselves in a room which is of the purest white, so white that it fairly shines its own glow, and that it is permeated by a million lights expanding above and around for an almost grotesque distance. Now suppose we turn a lamp on in the center of this fictional room- this new, small light will barely be visible. If we put this lamp in a dark room within which there is little light, then it will be more easily seen.

The darkness functions the same way. A void of darkness will be virtually invisible in a dark place but will be pronounced in a room which is well lit. Likewise, an "evil" man doing something "good" for perhaps the first time will be conspicuously good in this action, and a "good" man doing something "evil" for perhaps the first time equally so. Human understanding relies on these opposing terms and forces, but light and darkness are fairly similar and merely deal with the presence or absence of photons, or some symbolic representation thereof using the same terms. For the purposes of the occult the two should not be considered opposites but rather compliments with each causing the other to become more evident within a background of the so-called opposing force.

OCCULT PHILOSOPHY

The solar represents as well the power of the right hand path- the organized, male, logical, and public form of spiritual belief and practice.

Let us envision the sun and the moon as archetypes, so to speak. The sun represents the organized male right hand path, and the moon the disorganized female left hand path. This comparison is obvious- the sun is conspicuous in its presence, even on a cloudy day, and casts its light down when people tend to be awake and aware of it. The moon, meanwhile, "comes out" (is readily visible) at night and is often missed, and is gentler in form- it also sometimes becomes "empty" due to its position relative the sun and Earth and disappears altogether, much like the mystical left hand path often prefers anonymity or privacy.

If these two forces are seamlessly combined they create an occult power far above what either field can craft on its own. Magick is one part public and one part private. It is one part masculine and one feminine. Just as a fetus forms from a male potency and a female potency, so does magick truly become born when the two come together- this is a universal law with regards to creation, although the theory behind its existence differs from person and group to person and group.

Some believe this is because the cosmos has been artificially split into opposites during some fall out of a pure form, others that it is simply natural. Regardless, *as above so below* does not simply work in one direction, it works in both; except in a few rare cases of biological virgin birth in reptiles and amphibians, or cloning in plants, the perpetuation of life with all its force and potency relies upon a male and female force, bi-fold, coming together to form something new. This ties exactly in with the biological cycle itself, wherein in the most simplistic sense, a lower life form with a single year of life is planted, grows, ages, goes to seed and dies, and the resulting offspring are born the subsequent year after dormancy. A true love between the male and female forces will never allow either to truly die off altogether, and perhaps here we regard the Crowellian statement *love is the law.*

OCCULT PHILOSOPHY

THE IMPORTANCE OF DIVINE NUMBERS

Divine mathematics themselves must here be mentioned as well, for they are of high importance. Because we explain most phenomena within our physical existence in terms of that same finite set of decimals between zero and one which I already spoke of, mathematical principles, arbitrary as they may ultimately be, are of a highly symbolic nature as well.

There are many numbering systems in the world- those based on psychology, those based on mystic lore (especially from Judaism) and others based on nature- 666 is the most misunderstood because it variously represents Nero Caesar, Satan, the carbon atom, or any of a number of other things or names depending upon who you ask. In some systems this would be broken down by first adding the three sixes to eighteen, and then adding the one and eight to the number nine, reducing it. Nine would here be masculine and divine.

Richard Cavendish gives the explanation in his "Black Arts" that (in a general sense) the odd numbers are male and the even numbers female- his explanation here is well thought out but may be utterly without merit, for it seems to rely upon the observation (solely) that the odd numbers contain a digit in their center when represented as a picture, representing a male member, while the female numbers, as he envisions them, contain instead an opening in the middle, representing a vagina.

This oversimplification of the divine nature of mathematics is helpful only in understanding a few of these systems and a few of their meanings. I say, rather, that because the numbers involved are arbitrary they can represent almost anything, but here I revert to the vision of one and zero as the ultimate numbers within which all infinitely small sums are expressed in their finite mathematical form. One, therefore, represents infinity, and zero represents that which theoretically does not exist, for it is all about perspective.

OCCULT PHILOSOPHY

If, however, the intent is to use the base numbers within the Arabic numeral system (created by pagans before islam existed, so that the reader will understand that it is not an abrahamic system at all) then the numbers one through nine ought to be given some sort of meaning, while zero can also be quantified.

Zero represents an arbitrary minimum and nonexistent sum- however it also represents openness and receptivity- it is an undivided, unspoiled number just as one is undivided, and represents everything just as it represents the absence of anything at all- in this state, as nonexistence, all possibilities are present at once, and this arbitrary number cannot long truly exist before it is mutated into other forms. If nothingness, in a dimension, exists, it will spontaneously generate something, whereas if even so much as a single particle exists already it will be unable to generate anything further. We might consider this as akin to the dormant period within a plant's life cycle- it is dead, and gone, and withering under the snow, or in a drought during the dormancy of a dry season, but it *will* by definition return the next season. So too is zero, representative of emptiness, a temporary state of rest in between finite calculations of occult importance.

One represents the totality- infinity, and infinite existence. It is not so much in opposition here to the zero sum but rather again its compliment, for it represents the same thing in a different form. I say, that zero and one merely represent the respective empty and full phases of some divine totality, which is then further broken down over time into other sums. We start at zero, then existence occurs. When existence occurs, the sum approaches that divine one, and then degrades into entropy and shrinks back to zero again. One is the non-gendered number of totality- zero has no gendered existence because it is empty, but one represents the combined male and female, together, having just moments ago created existence. It is the number of intercourse itself, and of birth, just as zero is ascetic and represents the dead end of an ongoing cycle.

OCCULT PHILOSOPHY

The number two represents those same male and female forces split apart- the divine dichotomy and the number of understanding, for opposites are how we understand the reality we exist within. The number two is the purest number which can have a true physical existence separate from itself, for in the number one the self and the external are in essence the same thing- one represents all things together, two represents all things split apart, observing one another as separate entities, forgetting that they were moments ago part of the same divine whole. With the number two we get the first generative force which is capable of creating a separate being, and thus it must be female, for the female potency came first, and the female gives birth- if *as above so below* here holds true it must also be seen that the mother, not the father, primarily affects the birth in a biological manner, not just by virtue of carrying the child and nurturing it in utero, but also because of the passing of mitochondria, which are themselves a separate life form and one of the standards of advanced life. In Genesis it is claimed that the first female (or second female!) was responsible for the separation of the Eden, the divine whole- perhaps this is due to her motherhood. Upon generating a separate sentient being her own value was changed, not for the worse though, because it perpetuated life- perhaps their Jehovah was simply angered that the first couple made use of their sexual powers and denied their lord the right to merely clone them as he saw fit.

The number three must then be male, and represents the prime masculine potency. This is not because it happens to be odd, as some claim, but rather because it is the prime number following that divine female. The solar cults will tell you that Adam or some other man came first, but this is incorrect and the female comes first- this is the way it biologically and spiritually must be, regardless of whether the sun creates and the moon merely reflects light, which is why I deny that specific dichotomy that level of importance. Three represents the male force in its generative aspect, able to fertilize the female and perpetuate life in his own way. This is a number of wisdom in the solar, masculine sense. While two represents female, nurturing, spiritually pure love, three represents fatherly protection, and a physically protective nurturing.

OCCULT PHILOSOPHY

Four represents perpetuation of cycles- the mother two and father three have successfully perpetuated a second generation, and this will in turn advance over time back to the two and three respectively- and they must in order to create a new generation. Four is thus the number of the child, especially the female child, whereas five could be said to represent the male child. In a genetic manner, the X chromosome's value could be two, and the Y chromosome's value thus three- if the child is female their total number is four, but they will only allocate one of those two genetic alleles to the child they in the future themselves may have- the male and female being twain produces a male with the Y chromosome of the man passed on, but if he is passing an X chromosome he may oddly be passing one given to him by his mother rather than father, perpetuating a female chromosome despite himself being male; but the female can only pass the X chromosome on to her child and is more mathematically pure. The four is a stable number, and an inventive one able to be broken down into equal components; literally two twos.

Five is the number of physical perfection; it is prime and when doubled will result in the first possible number through this process that falls outside of the zero to nine set- literally, ten, forming the very basis of much of our finite mathematics. It is said to be a number for the male sexuality- an apt description since it contains this complexity- this is a purely physical matter. It is created from the pure female and male generative essences and must therefore be male, carrying both, for as I previously said the male is also able to pass a female chromosome thus resulting in the offspring being given the value of four. Five is a number of domination and conquest, being so purely male. It is an organized number- within our finite math we tend to use numbers ending in zero or five disproportionate to all others, allowing five an important position within accounting and other fiscal calculation. It is a number for wealth, a number for increase in the physical sense; for advancement and mental prowess. Five is the last number which stands alone. All further numbers are symbolically composed of the former.

OCCULT PHILOSOPHY

Six is a number representing camaraderie, it is metaphorically formed by a triplicate of divine female essences or a pair of divine male essences, and herein we see a further metaphor- the male is more limited than the female in its quantitative total; for where many females are gathered cooperation will tend to reign, but men will compete instead. In this manner the male dominant society will advance more quickly in a physical and technological manner, but the female society will be more ordered, oddly, *even though the male principle is that of organization.* The six thus has to have two meanings; it is the number of societal order if male, but it is also the number of societal order if female; the nature of this order is either male and physical or female and spiritual, but it will retain a similar meaning. This order is created when the female essence (two) instructs the divine daughter (four) or when two divine male essences (three) cooperate despite their own competitive nature. Therein lies the metaphysical meaning thereof. When this number is female, and composed of triplicate divine female entities, and is then tripled again, 666 is created- a number here in this system representing specifically a mystical order of pure feminine spirituality with all of its cooperative nature and references to naturalism itself, and to the world as a divine mother.

Seven is prime- it is not evenly composed like six is, of those of the same group but must be composed instead of an odd and even force. Here we could envision the divine total (one) conjoining with the ordered society (six) forming a combination basis between the divine and the physical. We could also say a divine female (two) has conjoined the male potency (five) or that the masculine (three) has instructed the daughter symbol (four.) In all such cases we have a conjoining of the spiritual female and physical male energies to a greater or lesser degree. Seven cannot stand alone but is a composition between other forces. Where a divine female has conjoined an ordered society bliss reigns, and where a father has instructed the daughter so too is there wisdom. Seven is thus the pure number of secular wisdom and the intelligence *behind* the order of six, as well as the rational counterpart of the divine feminine *and* the child.

OCCULT PHILOSOPHY

Eight is a number of the purest feminine energy. It can be made from a pair of female offspring or from four divine females, or by a divine female structuring two cooperating male offspring, in a symbolic sense. It is the most purely feminine number of all. Here lies another mystic secret- an ordered society formed by the male energy (six) may in turn be instructed or commanded by the divine female force (two) and thus take on an involuntary feminine nature, further structuring itself. Rome must be a society of eight- Romulus and Remus being male energies, each with a value of three, instructed by the divine she-wolf, with a value of two. When only one of the brothers was left the number reverted to five- bringing Roman wealth and power.

Nine is the final number which concerns us. It is the number of reincarnation and rebirth, for it is purely composed of the male and female child- the four and the five. It is not strictly male, but rather a final metaphysical force at the end of the cycle. It may also thus represent death, although this should be understood again as the temporary state. When nine degrades, it either reverts back into its components and a new generation, or represents the finality of a single incarnation before some other existence is regarded.

Thus in short the numbers are represented best as follows:

Zero: Emptiness and beginning.
One: The divine singularity.
Two: The divine/creative female.
Three: The divine/creative male.
Four: The female energy and daughter.
Five: The male energy and son.
Six: Social order and perfection.
Seven: Physical harmony and male cooperation or instruction.
Eight: Spiritual harmony and female cooperation or instruction.
Nine: Ending cycles, and rebirth.

OCCULT PHILOSOPHY

THE PLANETS

When we speak of planets we speak of things that have always been regarded as important within the occult. Not only are we regarding them from an alchemical stance (as representing various elements, or minerals, or substances, for example mercury) but also as bodies which represent the deities. In the Roman pantheon- based as it was on the Greek- we have of course Jupiter as Zeus and Mars as Aries, and so forth. This is all connected to the zodiac in use at the time and metaphorically represents different aspects of psychology and of the physical world- here as above so below is most evident of all, for they took the below and applied it to the above. In latter times, they attempted to claim the reverse had been true, and that the lords of the celestial realm had ordered the below in their image (many claim the same about all extant organized religious orders also.)

Before regarding their mystic alchemical nature and so forth, we must also note one important facet which is altogether forgotten by most. When we regard the cosmos not as a closed and limited system but rather one which is infinite in scope, and which is ultimately an open system, entropy itself becomes a temporary illusion. When science regards the cosmos as a closed and finite system it speculates that in ages to come the energy value will decline until there is little more than an endless expanse of cold void with some scattered, crumbled, frozen bodies floating haphazardly and without order. Finally, in the greater expanse of their linear, finite time, even these bodies will decay until the very subatomic particles holding them together degrade as well, eventually creating an abyss of absolute frozen waste- a nothingness so sheer and monumental as to render all human philosophy invalid by the very definitive nature of void, which they isolate, of course, from any possible creation process even without a basic understanding of how the cosmos were formed to begin with.

OCCULT PHILOSOPHY

If, however, we regard the cosmos as infinite in expanse, we see several concepts at work. First, outside energy from other universes or existences will interfere with the system they envision as closed, and second to this the lack of uniqueness behind what we see as creation (call it the big bang, as it were) is removed; another such event could occur at any time, in any location. Perhaps this process wasn't random to begin with and the pull of so much energy and matter fuming out from the central point from which the universe originally came, will be manipulated in some way by this pulling and simultaneously generate a new universe when the old one has become too decayed. In turn, all of the bodies composing the old will find themselves eventually absorbed into some other semi-closed finite universe elsewhere after being fired through the void for a billion years or so beyond their date of heat death. If this is the case than entropy as we understand it also does not exist.

In fact even within our imagined closed system the expanse of time involved is so great that there is more than ample time for any dead body to be impacted by another, perhaps driven into orbit around a newer star and thus able to be revived again anew. If we however imagine the system is open and not finite, then this is not just a possibility but eventually a certainty.

Entropy thus we can regard as nonsense; we observe it temporarily, but if we envision even this planet's age as being a twenty four hour period, we have existed for only but a second of its total time spent existing. We are incapable, in these temporal forms we inhabit, of actually understanding more than a brief moment in time, and our best guesses are literally just that- but all of the scientists and mathematicians that pretend their mathematical systems are objective are misapplying their very good knowledge to fruitless ends. Entropy, in an open system, *does not exist* in an objective sense and when we observe it we observe it only temporarily, This is also the case with decay. One life form becomes entropic and the same energy it contains is used by others which consume it to resist entropy. This is universal cannibalism and the cosmos practice it also. *As above so below.*

OCCULT PHILOSOPHY

The planets move in their cycles in a seemingly infinite manner- however over the great expanse of time they too will die- the sun will expand and destroy the inner planets, then explode and collapse, roasting the outer planets, and sending the solar system into disarray- perhaps one of them will be lucky and be shielded by one of the inner which will block a direct hit from the resulting cataclysm, but the solar system will be "dead" for a very long time- the Hindu measure their time in the hundreds of millions of years and such cycles perhaps are related to this- for in time the system will be absorbed by some other body- or at least the matter contained therein will be. The dead planets will be reborn, and once again slowly will be filled with energy, and become dynamic systems.

When we say alive or dead in a planetary sense we are mostly speaking in terms of "more or less sterile" for indeed many have no actual life on them- but they have weather, they have wind and storms and water, and rain and steam. They often have volcanic and seismic activity. Their moons circulate around them much as ours does, although any life they do contain is not obvious to us at this time. I will speak here of Mars, where even science is anxiously studying the seemingly barren surface because the scientists have revealed that it contains water, decomposed soils, and remnants of what were once bodies of water which circulated, so too does it have evidence of past vulcanism amongst other things- in this way it seems likely we will find that life, if it does not exist there now, at least did in the past and was snuffed out by temporary entropy. It even contains trace amounts of gaseous substances which are normally created through organic means.

In the more literal sense I claim that the cosmos are teeming with life. We tend to regard the expanse of space as largely a vacuum with a few rocky bodies floating around some sterile solar bodies with our one lonely planet the only one populated by any life- yet the same scientists that believe this also say life arose by chance through abiogenesis and that all that was required was a dynamic planet with weather and the precursors to organic molecules which then created life from non-life through randomized processes.

OCCULT PHILOSOPHY

The fact that they have to presume that this random event was almost infinitesimally unlikely in order to not presume it has happened elsewhere because of the sheer number of stars and planets that exist is mildly amusing. It got even funnier not long in the past when new technology allowed us to glimpse smaller bodies out in the far reaches of space, and we now know that our planet is "about average" in size and probably about average in composition; the odds of life are far higher in this situation than in the recent past when we imagined most planets were gigantic and (possibly) less likely to spawn bacteria or other life forms.

I say that life is infinite and immortal- it will never truly end, even when the universe decays, as their theories suggest it will; even this is just a theory and may not be true, but let us suppose that it is- surely out there, right at this very moment, there are extra terrestrials looking for us as much as we are for them- this is a comforting thought. Many occultists ignore this sort of material and focus on their orbs and grimoires, without regarding the likely possibility that at some future date we may become privy to a whole host of spiritual knowledge sent from afar, perhaps electronically or perhaps through a direct visitation by beings more advanced than ourselves. Perhaps they will see man as little more than a rudimentary sovereign being the way we see apes, and will declare our planet a nature reserve in order to protect us, and when they visit, they will make no attempt at communication because to them we will merely be interesting animals to be gawked at and satirized. Here again as above so below- we have to assume that the logic we use towards "lesser" beings will be similar to that used towards us should we receive such visitation- in which case we might imagine a carnivorous alien that enjoys cooking and eating humans because to them we are nothing more than a convenient and helpless food source whose own technological level does not allow the human to resist.

OCCULT PHILOSOPHY

Now we will delve into the more traditional alchemical meanings behind the planets- for it is an interesting if abstract concept.

The sun of course is not a planet but is typically associated with gold- this makes sense given its color, but also because of its associations with increase and thus wealth- the sun increases the harvest, the gold increases one's wealth.

The moon is associated with silver- again the color appears to be at play here, however those of ancient times did not seem to understand that the moon simply reflects the light of the sun, which they had already labeled as having to do with gold rather than silver. Perhaps this was however a willful subjugation thereof- for silver is often likened as second to gold. Oddly enough, despite this, within alchemy the concept of turning things *into* gold was of importance, and many theorized that other materials were just corrupted gold that required extensive and elaborate purification. How this corruption occurred was, seemingly, up for debate.

Mercury naturally associates with the same element mercury, called *quicksilver*. Mercury was extraordinarily important in all of its forms within alchemy, although it is also extremely toxic in most of these forms and probably led to some degree of madness in many of the folks attempting to boil or otherwise treat it as an alchemical addition.

Venus is likened to copper and Jupiter to tin. When these two are smelted down and forged together they create bronze- which at the time was still of vast importance and to the early alchemists of antiquity was important because iron at the time was prohibitively expensive to extract (in fact in earlier antiquity bronze was the strongest alloy available.) Here we might chuckle and say that Jupiter (Zeus) and Venus (Aphrodite) somehow combined their abilities together- this would make some sense since both godly conquest and romantic lust were involved with the battles raging during the bronze age.

OCCULT PHILOSOPHY

Mars is associated with iron. Another apt comparison given the aspect of war carried by both. Iron continues to be of great importance within war to this day, for the crafting of weaponry and armor, amongst other things. Perhaps it is the slightly reddish color of this planet that likens it to iron, rusted as it were as an impure ore waiting to be refined. How strange, that this metal, which for so long was so valued for the crafting of weaponry, will degrade upon even casual exposure to the air or water (through which it will oxidize and, for most mechanical purposes, become useless.)

Saturn is associated with lead. This alchemical substance along with the mercury so often used would surely have led to health problems as well. As a soft metal, it was added often to other substances for the easy crafting of cups and plates, as well as every other utensil. We get the classic image of the leaden spear of Bellerophon slaying the chimera by waiting until it breathes fire, then thrusting it down its throat, choking the beast.

Although we do not notice it on a day to day basis these celestial bodies and others are pulling our planet at all times, and pulling on one another- objects flying through space are perturbed by these bodies out of their "normal" trajectories on a constant basis. Celestial materials are prized for use in the making of blades and amulets- I have seen knives and daggers made from smelted iron taken from meteorites, or carved directly when the fragment was large enough. These beautiful blades would be exceptionally useful for the making of athames, at least if the skill of the smith is high enough to work with material which tends to have such an uneven shape. Much as we see the prevalence of a large crystal- quartz usually- in a stave or wand, a fragment of meteor has a different meaning, for it was out there in the cold void for extreme lengths of time, and we must think of the material it has absorbed over time from moving near these various bodies, surrounded each and every one by their own debris from the occasional impact over the great length of time.

OCCULT PHILOSOPHY

OCCULT PHILOSOPHY

THE CYCLE OF THE MAN

There are also cycles involved with the human being- more specifically with all biological beings as a whole, but here it is the human that concerns us.

A human being is not very much unlike a plant. They are both composed (literally) of the same dead matter arranged into what a secular scientist would believe to be a mechanized arrangement. Both beings contain water, both contain carbon- in fact they essentially contain identical substances which merely have been arranged into different compositions and orders.

That is at least the secular explanation of what must be said to actually be a spiritual concept. Had you told a scientist three centuries ago that there was no intrinsic difference between the two beings- a human and an eggplant- they'd have seen you locked up as a lunatic. However, it is now accepted that this is the case. But, if we look to the more occult thinkers of the world, we see that this claim was already made long ago.

Firstly, that even Paracelsus-derived medical lore from many centuries ago regarded all substances as fitting essentially into hot and cold as categories; this oversimplification of medicine and matter nonetheless has a metaphoric truth behind it, because for the first time the claim was made that there was interchangeability between substances that for so long after were considered substantially separate. If we look at a man and then at the eggplant we say they aren't the same, but although Paracelsus got his categories wrong his basic idea was correct- the two are made up of the same particles. Even the new age of occultism (and to a lesser degree the shamanism it is so often based off of) references this in the concept of a universal energy permeating even the nonliving objects of the cosmos- rocks and so forth, as well as life that nonetheless has no volition or mentality such as trees or grass. The occult was indeed centuries ahead of modern science on the subject.

OCCULT PHILOSOPHY

Anthroposophy and Theosophy have similar explanations for this. Rudolf Steiner was perhaps the wisest man in the Victorian era within the occult and noted in his works that there were multiple levels of existence in which the biological were able to act. First, that primitive life such as a plant was able to change nonliving force into living force. After this comes lower life- animals and primitive man, so to speak, or uncivilized man. These manifest a second level of energy, that is the etheric capability to dream, to see in the minds' eye and so forth- inventiveness and inner sight. In the current civilized level it goes beyond this dim recognition of self and external and becomes an astral level of higher mentality. He then posits a future level in which the human has almost ascended mentally and gained additional capabilities- to recognize things in a true critical manner.

Steiner prefaces this by observing it to be the reverse of tribal or racial memory- that is that more primitive humans were able to mentally remember events they themselves as singular beings were not part of, because they had not yet attained an externalized mentality- when they did, that tribal capability was lost. This appears to fit in further with biology when we consider a flock of birds (undoubtedly lower than even primitive tribal man had been) able to simultaneously move in tandem in any direction during flight, or a school of fish doing the same thing. They have a sort of collective mind- the same as a colony of ants or many other lower life forms.

The secular scientist would claim this is because these beings are more mechanical and exhibiting what may be termed an advanced form of taxis- they are merely reacting to minute perturbations of the magnetic field perhaps, or slight temperature changes, or a breeze. The occultist might surmise that this oversimplifies it and that the mechanical actually follows the mental or spiritual- that is that such beings exhibit this mechanical trait because they are not fully able to externalize the world beyond their own egotistical sensory experiences, which nonetheless perform as a collective. If this is the case then science is technically right, but is misattributing cause and effect.

OCCULT PHILOSOPHY

The period in women is another example of such cycles and phenomena within the human race- although the same happens in other species as well. This menstrual period is notoriously unstable and is capable of disappearing altogether, or delaying itself with seemingly no reason. It changes in flow, it causes mood disruptions.

However it is a necessary aspect of the female body- the birthing process itself is intrinsic in the function of life. If it were not for the painful process of birth there would be no human race. The abrahamist ascribes to this pain negativity- that is the tale of course of Eve sinning in the garden and eating the fruit of knowledge, thus being punished by having her pain multiplied.

There are several things to be said here; first that this abrahamic story actually comes from Sumeria and that the original tale was less masculine in form- Eve was not punished but rather applauded by those who desired to unleash the full potential of the human race, which appear to have been enslaved prior to this event by a semi-malevolent race of very tall humanoid aliens or demons as workers to mine gold. In these same stories Adam is Adamu and Lilith is Lilitu. The eating of the fruit that causes this birthing disruption is not seen here as negative except by the enslaving angels, which quickly realize they can no longer inhabit the planet because a sentient race native to it now has the intelligence necessary to wage war (which they appear to have had little concept of or possibly a deep moral opposition to.)

Likewise this is mostly just the Judaist manner of explaining why birth hurts- to them, it seems, the presence of pain during the process must naturally mean that the process was itself fallen and corrupted, for they had difficulty (presupposing man to have been incarnated in glory at first) in understanding why their lord would require such pain for what was to them an ongoing cycle creating new life.

OCCULT PHILOSOPHY

The concept of no birth without blood comes in here. Existence, life, perpetuating and preserving it, is a struggle- the Germanic Order recognized this as well, with the concept of eternal *kampf* or eternal struggle, which purified a race or a nation or an individual. Indeed, this is merely an anthropic noting of what is regarded as basic biology. Survival of the fittest- that which is strong, and desirable (at least in a given era or situation) tends to be preserved, and that which is weaker will often be destroyed, either because it becomes diseased or is predated upon, or because it exhibits a lower reproductive capability.

In this way we might not see the pain of the woman's period or of birth as a negative thing but rather a natural expression of the struggle for survival. We do not see, for example, a plant suffering because it releases seed (at least if it is a perennial) but the plant also has no mentality or volition and is unable to feel pain in the manner we recognize as such. Funnily, it is now supposed that plants exhibit what might be considered rudimentary "feelings" through the release of pheromones to one another when eaten, or through chemical reactions when destroyed.

Embryonic stages are taught in any competent introductory level course in biology. The embryo of a human over time goes from a mostly formless mass of cells, to resembling at first lower life forms (including having a tail) and finally becomes more or less human in the third trimester- before this it bears a remarkable resemblance to lower life forms which have completed their own life cycle and are already adults. Science regards this as proof of evolution; so too do I, but I also see it as proof of the interchangeability of life forms, lending its way to things like reincarnation and *kampf*- this latter I will expound upon.

OCCULT PHILOSOPHY

Within evolution science typically regards different species as separate competitors for the same resources. It says this, even after telling the truth- essentially that all of these life forms came from one primordial source- a bacterium in a pond of scum or a chemotroph dwelling in some mile-deep chasm full of thermal vents billions of years ago, or some other forsaken location where life began. If this be true, then no matter how differentiated two species may be they are of the same single lineage.

In this case we might see evolution not as a struggle *between species* but rather a struggle by *all species* to improve one another over time, to purify their own traits, to compete solely to show off this singular lineage' own improvements and capabilities. To this singular lineage it does not matter if a species dies off entirely, so long as it has done so because it was replaced by another. And it will be replaced; for no niche able to be inhabited will be uninhabited- whether we're speaking of the porous soils of a steaming, active volcano, or a deep sea sediment layer, or a cave three miles underground where not a single photon penetrates.

That is, the *kampf* is real, and merely being misused by racialists or else misunderstood by its proponents. It is real, but it is not competition between species, it is a purification process in which spiritually aware and biologically mechanical life forms steadily change one another and put pressure on one another to do so. The fact that being killed "hurts" or being diseased is discomforting matters little from the perspective of the *kampf* because even if a billion humans or a whole species dies out entirely it did so because its biological ability to preserve itself was too limited to cope with stress. Even the universe itself tests these lineages of life forms, constantly bombarding cosmic bodies with chunks of debris or solar explosions- at the end of the era of mega-fauna, as the dinosaurs in their dim recognition of reality looked upon the rock hurtling towards the planet, not one of them understood they were about to face the greatest test Earth had faced since the dawn of life when the next major extinctions occurred.

OCCULT PHILOSOPHY

This eternal struggle takes on separate meaning depending upon what it's applied to. If we apply it to pure science- to actual biology and evolution, then it is neither moral nor immoral because these concepts are created by humans and are artificial (except wherein they improve survivorship, exactly as a physical mutation might.) If, however, we attempt to apply this reasoning to strictly artificial human machinations the system breaks down, because the artificial is seeking to apply the natural to itself while retaining its own vestitures of artifice. This bastardization of biology has been the root of much suffering, especially in the eugenics era.

The human embryo is passing through stages in which it resembles other life forms because those life forms are the same thing as the human itself- the only difference between a bacterium and a human is that they have differentiated over time in order to fill more niches. Imagine a world solely comprised of chemotrophic bacteria. They are only able to take advantage of a few energy sources- and then photosynthesis arises and the sun is used for energy. We now know that some fungi and bacteria use radiation as an energy source also. And then we have detritus-ingesting life forms that remove dead matter and cycle it back into living matter. We have then at last carnivorous life forms which predate on the others. This last category seems aberrant here- the others are not harming other life forms for their own well being, but yet without the carnivores there is one less stress on them to improve their own biological state. Carnivores are thus not morally reprobate (vegans take heed) but rather form an important part of the natural spiritual and physical process of improvement and advancement. Evolution regards change over time not as advancement but merely as change- however it *is* improvement in response to specific external stimuli. What better way for a divine plan to operate except through competition? Even in the human artifice of production and economy, competition has crushed all other forms of production; capitalism reigns supreme specifically because it is the most efficient and the most dynamic, as opposed to systems which stifle innovation and protect the weak which produce nothing.

OCCULT PHILOSOPHY

Even the completely secular atheist should note that this is true; the species we observe competing do not do so in order to destroy one another utterly; what would be the point of destroying your own food source? Rather, they seek to predate to preserve themselves, with both sides steadily changing over time in response to one another as well as to other stimulus. It matters little whether this was divinely designed or naturally designed. The occultist doesn't even need to think about which of these two is "true" as long as the natural observation is correct.

A human being is born. Having passed through multiple embryonic stages and "become human-like" after a few months have passed, it is then born, and the moment it is born the struggle begins. The process of becoming truly human requires more than that this infant persevere to a reproductive age, for as sentient beings we have further capabilities- philosophy and critical thinking design our entire reality, for we experience the external in our own terms, unlike lower life forms able to externalize but merely observe. We alone, above all other creatures, do not simply see reality, but *make* reality. The occultist might take this to a level even further above that and say our very mental imagery affects the dimensions above ours- I agree; but it also affects those below by creating limitless realities in which other beings now exist. This special capability can be proven only on a theoretical basis, for as I said we cannot directly observe these lower dimensions.

The human being then moves through life, maturing and aging and gaining experience. If we apply the biological principle of adaptation and improvement to the spiritual (*as above so below*) then we may say we are here in order to simply experience and think, and to craft a future reality for ourselves solely because *we are able to do so*. I reject the moralists who say that it is necessary to behave in one specific manner- say asceticism or even hedonism for hedonism's sake- rather I say that such a sentient being is called on to make their own decisions, to become their own monarch and leader, and to gain what experiences they wish.

OCCULT PHILOSOPHY

Understanding then begins when we realize that there is a disconnect between the biological and the spiritual with regards to our own health either as individuals or as species.

On a strictly physical basis- that which all governments care about- it is best to limit the will of individuals somewhat to prevent them from harming one another. Taken to its unfortunate modern extreme this manifests as overt regulation of behaviors and choices which actually harm nobody but which some (oddly spiritual) moralist felt were negative. We see this all the time, from psychotropics to sexuality to business regulations. Conglomerates of fallible humans called governments are empowered to do what is right and subsequently spend most of their existence making decisions far more ridiculous and harmful than the people at large even in an anarchic state would have made.

On a more spiritual basis it is more important that freedom reign. The notion that any moral system, however positive, is superior to others is patent nonsense and usually derived from the belief that some divine tyrant exists that punishes you when you die. Nonsense, I say; such a being wouldn't care one bit what you did as long as you did what was natural to you and harmed nobody else in the process of fulfilling your own desires. This is the true nature of man; he is free to make his own choices, and must take responsibility for his own actions. Heavy-handed government and totalitarianism are the direct polar opposite (insofar as opposites actually exist) to a divine, natural existence where humans celebrate their bodies and souls and minds equally and in which good and bad ideas compete in philosophical discourse, eventually purifying philosophy itself. Long gone are the days of true freedom, although perhaps part of this is our own fault for misusing our minds to abuse the planet as a whole- this action *will* have a reaction sooner or later, which will be our downfall and likely plunge us backwards several centuries. You cannot eat money.

OCCULT PHILOSOPHY

THE CYCLE OF THE SEASONS AND THEIR CONNECTION TO THE SPIRITUAL

The seasons of the year, at least as we experience them on our planet, also have an effect upon our spiritual understanding. First, let us remember that this too is an arbitrary observation which is true predominantly only on our one planet. Were we to colonize Mars the seasons experienced there even with extensive terraforming would be vastly different than our own- the cold would be colder, the hot hotter, the days of different length, the seasons as well different, possibly more erratic. What does this say about spiritual advancement, were humans to take root there and diverge from those here on Earth? These are questions the occult and the philosophical must discuss, for in time the human race is likely to take hold there and elsewhere out of curiosity or necessity.

The occult energy present during each season differs. Here I will differentiate between several of the major biomes and climates on the planet, for the surroundings have a definitive effect upon the occult nature of ritualism and spiritual belief. First, let us regard the temperate climate that involves most of North America and Europe, as well as other locations between the tropics and polar regions.

Labeling spring as the first season is arbitrary also- you could just as easily start your calendar in June but the spring to winter cycles used in most are superior in explaining spiritual concepts. With spring you have renewal- the world has been "destroyed" by the cold in a Ragnarok-style yearly purge of annual plant life, and the barren world begins to live again anew, at least for life forms which survived the snow and ice.

In spring the generative force is at its peak- it's not coincidence that the fertility rites that were later turned into modern Easter are a springtime sex ritual. The only amusing part to this is that it's most fervently celebrated by children of a prepubescent age despite its overwhelming sexual overtones. Adults of a sexually mature age typically don't run around collecting eggs on this festive day, but they might be busy mating and producing more children who will.

OCCULT PHILOSOPHY

In spring the positive aspect of ritualism is very much in play along with the hedonistic. True spirituality here is the recognition of life itself and sentience as well- it is a time for more pure celebration, because the sun is "returning" and life is springing up around us. The human being here finds their first spirituality- for it is this same celebratory hedonism. To the child, all of those rituals in a church are boring and they would much rather wander the woods pretending to fight goblins; this should not be seen as play so much as mental awakening- imagination plays a key role in magick, and it's not clear why so many people in this world are so miserable as to try and rob the young of their imaginations, shoving them into school or elsewhere where all they are taught is *what* to think rather than *why* we regard the world as we do. The lack of critical thinking imparted to them, the lack of regard for imagination and play, the lack of teaching them to be their own god, in a sense, is hideous when seen from an occult background.

In the summer spirituality is not the same. It is a more potent and anthropic force. In the summer things have matured and are at their physical prime- in this state the man in his own summer of life leaves behind the imagination for imagination's sake and begins to delve into deeper pondering about nature. The summer of nature and that of a man coincide, although they are only symbolically connected.

The man here will focus the spiritual on his own self- that is, to adapt the spiritual to his own adult desires. Here lies the root of magick which involves things which we would not ascribe to children, such as sexual ritualism or something of that nature. Man attempts to project his force, his desire, his goals into the spiritual realm when he is in this period, just as in nature competition is at its peak and every species is attempting to predate, pollinate, reproduce, grow, and spread to the best of its ability in a wild genetic free-for-all orgy of competition. Physically this is when the man becomes most motivated as well, at least most humans will do so.

OCCULT PHILOSOPHY

The autumn is a time of dying for most life forms of an annual nature- the frost comes, the seeds are sown and become the next generation. Here, the human begins to apply the spirituality they have found and developed to the world around them. No longer as in spring do they experience without bias, and no more do they apply the spiritual to themselves as much; here they are applying it to the outside world.

Much as the plant in autumn is now filling the world around it with its physical progeny, here the human is filling the world with their spiritual progeny, perpetuating their own bias and belief, whatever it may be. At this point they are regarded as elder and often listened to as a source of wisdom. We get the vision of the aging wizard or mage as much as the politician, now in his or her sixties, making decisions supposedly based on a near lifetime of wisdom. In many cases this wisdom is itself flawed; the result of misapplication of learning in younger years, or of bias which is invalidated, or by their own egotistical ideations; the source of misery coming from such self appointed leaders, however, is less about their egotistical attempts to exert power, but rather the attempt to exert it irrationally and wrongfully, based on principles which are themselves flawed. If the plant is afflicted, the progeny may be afflicted- if the man is afflicted in his spirit, the progeny of his spiritual attempts will be equally so. A pastor in the church stands and delivers sermons which misrepresent his own dogma, an aged, wizened former flower child is now in her sixties and has grown bitter and disdainful- herein is the flaw of man's spirituality, for it often comes itself from flawed beliefs.

Winter is the ending of the human cycle and the natural cycle. Now all is growing barren and cold- when winter comes, we do not say that it will be cold forever and the world is dying, we say simply that soon it will be spring and flowers will grow again. Most people don't apply this same concept to what they imagine is a linear sentience; the atheist assumes that when they physically die they stop existing as an ego able to experience anything. The abrahamist imagines they will never again be physical beings but will be in some other realm. Even believers in reincarnation imagine that extremely long cycles eventually end in some enlightened state.

OCCULT PHILOSOPHY

However, as above so below; the cycle does not end. Those who hope for heaven have forsaken heaven in this world and in others. Those that imagine there is nothing beyond the grave are mistaken and will cause themselves pain in believing such a farcical thing. Those that hope for an end to reincarnation cycles and the attainment of some non-physical enlightened state are perhaps the most fooled of all; they understand time isn't linear yet they try to make it so.

In some eastern paths the process of devachan or something similar is regarded as temporary, the ebb and flow of existence is exceedingly long, and there are cycles within cycles here which are never ending; we may regard their specific claims as opinion only but the principle is correct; there will never, in this open system, come a time at which the ego is completely destroyed, for it exists infinitely in other dimensions. A skilled occultist may create whatever thought-forms they wish there, to experience once this body they currently use has died and decayed.

In winter, the plant is not truly dead- in fact it is more alive than ever and merely hibernating. The plant was once singular- it was one single living thing, that experienced a single, finite existence and did so passively- it doesn't even have a sentience or a mental capability. When winter has finally ended, when the hibernation cycle is complete, more than one plant is likely to spawn from the seed it scattered- sometimes with help indeed from a sentient being that knew how to cause it to grow.

How much more, then, do sentient beings promulgate their future existence beyond the physical grave? If a life form as simple as a plant can create hundreds of clones of itself every year, how much more can we perpetuate our own spiritual form when we are temporarily untethered from a physical body? The very genetics of a clonal species of plant will be identical to the parent- many self pollinate to begin with- and even if the result was cross pollinated, it will contain nothing that was not donated from its parental lineage. It remains a part of them.

OCCULT PHILOSOPHY

In winter, the human being reflects upon their life, both physical and spiritual. They ponder their actions during life. Perhaps they find that they did more or less what they wished to do and needed to do, and they will be content. In this end of the cycle they feel fulfilled, not afraid, although they almost all hesitate at the end and ponder the nature of death itself, questioning what will happen on that fateful night when they do not wake up was the sun rises.

It could be that they realize (with horror) that most of their life was, to them, a waste of time. That they accomplished little of what they wanted, that they accomplished nothing at all. They become frightened and mentally unhinged, because upon questioning their beliefs and actions they find little of a concrete nature there to base their death on. It isn't death itself that frightens, it is what lies beyond; to imagine a void of nonexistence, or eternal Hell, is frightening to one who believes in such things.

Here there is true wisdom in two parts. First, this death is the end only of a single cycle. You *will* persist elsewhere; both in the form you have recently experienced and in other forms- in fact, an infinite number of incarnations has created a series of physical and nonphysical states which range from liquefied, atomized matter to various physical forms of a sentient nature.

Second, the goal of one who has achieved this great age, and who looks back in pain at their life, which they imagined was wasted is simply to cast aside such fear. Since the cycle is just one of a limitless number, it ultimately *doesn't matter* what you did during your life beyond enjoying it, at least if we regard it as primarily physical. In the spiritual sense, it is not the same; your goal was to promulgate the beliefs that seemed good to you. If you promulgated no belief at all, so be it- for you will be back yet again and again.

OCCULT PHILOSOPHY

The best state that one can possibly inhabit is one of eternal spring; without bias, merely experiencing the world, with little or no expectation and with no regard for reality beyond a tip of the hat to the very word. An occultist who embraces the power of spring will never fail, for they will remain ambitious yet they will not become tethered to one limited view, and they will remain curious about all that they experience. They will become powerful in their mind, because they will both think critically and enjoy life- and the occultist in this state will not become bogged down with moral beliefs which would stifle their development. To the springtime occultist all is possible and nothing off limits. This is true spirituality.

The occultist embracing the power of summer will exude charisma but this will be a degraded egoism. They will seek to affect reality, but will ultimately lack the ability to effectively influence and change themselves. The best way to sum up this paradox is that *they will possess the ability to change the external even when changing the self would be easier or better for their development.* Most occultism falls into this category or the next.

The occultist embracing the power of autumn will exude a fallacious wisdom, for they have become a shape shifter of sorts. They may be able to change others through their teachings but only if they have already learned to change themselves. Paradoxically *they find it simple to steel themselves in their beliefs but if they are flawed they will be spiritually harmful to themselves and others.* A great many charlatan spiritualists fall into this trap.

The occultist living in winter will become anxious and constantly seek to assure themselves of their own existence. Attempts to achieve physical immortality always spawn from this- and it has led even those with no occult beliefs at all astray. Seeking this physical immortality (often through physical egotism) they abandon reality altogether and doom themselves to be ever wanting and ever unfulfilled. Here lies the man who has spent his entire life hoarding wealth only to end up on his death bed unable to even get up to walk to the bank and check his account, or the great warrior in old age who has no strength left and finds himself helpless; this is the worst of all states

OCCULT PHILOSOPHY

That is to say, that there are four basic tenets within the seasons as they apply to spiritual concepts.

In the spring, the human says "I am experiencing" and experiences the spiritual and physical with little to no regard for anything connected to it. These moral or physical arguments are meaningless because they are ignored. There is no "impossible" in this quarter of existence, because things are naturally experienced and any philosophical musings and ruminations spawned will be those of agnostic curiosity rather than those of objective resolve. This is symbolized by the child.

In the summer, the human says "I am doing" and focuses the spiritual on the self, manipulating the former in accordance with desire. In this way, they will change the world according to their will- sometimes for the better sometimes the worse. Often they inadvertently do the same to themselves, also to their benefit or detriment. Because of their bias, they only *think* they know what is best for themselves. This is symbolized by the man.

In the fall, the human says "It is doing" and recognizes their mortality. They focus the spiritual on the external and attempt to further manipulate it to leave a legacy or name behind. Should they fail, they exist this quarter and for them a cold winter awaits. Because of their bias, they only *think* they know what is best for others. This is symbolized by the king.

In the winter, the human says "It is finished and I am finished" and introspects upon the spiritual, the physical, and upon their own life which is now mostly done. They then seek repentance for a life they presume to have been lived incorrectly, or they feel fulfilled and at peace. In some schools of thought this intrinsically affects the outcome after death. Because of their bias they may *think* they have failed some objective measure. This is symbolized by the tomb.

OCCULT PHILOSOPHY

OCCULT PHILOSOPHY

THE CYCLE OF THE AGES

We can see both smaller and larger cycles at play here which must be noted by the occultist much the same way the movement of planets and other celestial bodies are noted; for they affect the energy available for ritualism, and affect the psychology, and thus affect the rituals performed even further.

Over a million years ago some primitive human grasped a sharp rock and noted its efficacy in killing animals, or perhaps in gutting them to prepare for eating. This primitive being was nonetheless aware enough to compare its use to other, less sharp instruments, and decided that something about its shape made it more effective at this use. Taking a chunk of obsidian in one hand, the being smashed it with a rock until he or she was able to hammer it into the crude form of the first hand ax.

This seems like an elementary concept, for any of us could form a similar obsidian or flint instrument easily if we wanted to- the skill involved is negligible although I've seen anthropologists recreate it and pretend it's a monumental task of learning. However, when this was done for the first time, this primitive human or hominid (the two might as well be classed as the same thing in different forms) made a leap forwards from the era in which man was mostly apelike, into a further era in which man manipulated foreign objects for his own benefit.

We have to wait hundreds of thousands of years beyond that first primitive action to find other remnants of similar tools- flint chips used specifically for cutting, spear points, and so forth. Man develops fire, and the first stone age cultures- for cultures they were- begin. We tend to look back on these primitive people and consider them uncultured the way we might regard a chimpanzee or an orangutan, but they must have had some form of crude gestural or vocal communication in order to have taught one another to make tools.

OCCULT PHILOSOPHY

I predict that these beings already had a sort of spiritual belief system- Marx believed that early man was a communal creature with no ownership system but when we regard the remains of early humans- at least those later who were able to organize things- we see instead the rudiments of a social order which partly stressed personal ownership. Some of the first cities were arranged in almost beehive-style clusters, which seems communal enough until you consider that most or all apartments therein contained their own hearth and their own tribal style remains- it seems they interned the dead within their own homes, storing the skulls especially there and using them for ritual purposes.

This first stage of organized culture could only have thought to do so if there was already some sense of importance to these remains and to personal or familial ownership of goods; so I say that Marx was wrong and that instead early man exhibited a culture which stood for a fusion of religious and social order, rather than communalism, which was based not on "tribe" but on "lineage." Much as all creatures on the planet are just highly differentiated versions of the same primordial life form that change in response to stimuli, the concept amongst humans of familial lineage has played a role in all cultures, and that, too, is merely a differentiation between beings which share the same genetic precursor back somewhere along the line.

We can scarcely comprehend the sort of rituals which would have been concocted by these early humans- envision as it were ceremony bereft of any modern understanding of symbolism, psychology, or the elements. Theirs would have been powerful, for they would have been almost entirely naturalistic in form; much like, as I discussed, occultism modeled after spring. These days, it is all modeled after summer or autumn as seasons, but in those days of old people were indeed childlike, and this led to their advances; every flame, every light, was something curious to them, to be thought about long and hard. It's not inconceivable that these humans were already experimenting with the world around them and were able to understand cause and effect to a degree.

OCCULT PHILOSOPHY

I have spoken of one theory which I believe in time will be adopted as truth by archaeology. It is my belief that advanced human civilizations existed before the last ice age and were wiped out by glaciation- unfortunately at this time any remains of such a culture would have been plowed deep into the northern soils by those same glaciers which would have crushed all of their buildings and reduced them to pebbles, and they are now covered by mountain ranges and valley soil sediments.

Mostly we regard man as having been developed only upon the founding of Egypt. This is a purely abrahamic belief, for Sumeria predates it by several thousand years. The christians and jews for a long time have considered the Sumerians little more than blood drinking heretical pagans who built a ziggurat and promptly sank into the steppe never to be seen again. This is folly.

Science has yet to create a solid explanation for all of these megaliths, particularly why such similar figures exist all across the world. There are pyramids in Egypt, yes, but also in what is now China, Brazil, the Azores off of Europe, and elsewhere- there were gigantic earth mounds built in the center of what is now the continental United States and nobody wants to talk about them.

However the occult knows full well what these are- the pyramid may be a simplistic geometric form but it would have been senseless for (as science imagines) primitive people barely able to raise an agricultural surplus to have spent much of their effort building megaliths. Rather, they would have needed substantial organization and advanced tools to do so, and they were not built by slaves, but involved a large scale community effort. We now know, for certain, that the old testament is incorrect when it makes the fantastic claim that jewish slaves were employed to craft some of the larger pyramids in Egypt. They were, in fact, built by Egyptians themselves largely because during the dry season there was no other work to be done. In order to get their share of the stored surplus of food they labored in this manner, and the Pharaohs thus rewarded the work of their people with the surplus.

OCCULT PHILOSOPHY

The pyramid has additional meaning- the vast corpus of its matter is connected to the earth, and only one terminal point reaches upwards, pointing into the cosmos. The Egyptians seem to have regarded the point in the sky at which stars and so forth seemed to swirl around as a sort of portal of energy, perhaps the same one they reference as where the dead flew into the next life should the be found worthy to do so. It makes sense, then, that they would have built pyramids even though some appear not to have been used as tombs, notably the great pyramid. I theorize that its occult purpose was deeper- it was a communal structure in which normal citizens were brought, rituals performed, and their bodies then removed after the spirit had enough time to move up the structure. The shape was thus meant to show them the way to move- upwards into that same spiritual void.

Perhaps the latter day pyramids without permanent entombed occupants were meant for this purpose- perhaps towards the end of these specific periods of time, the people wondered why they didn't get the same treatment their rulers did. It could be that a benevolent pharaoh decreed that all bodies should thus be given this opportunity at glory, or perhaps the people threatened to overthrow the ruling class if they did not do so.

So the first step of man's infant move towards the spiritual was merely his capability to manipulate foreign matter to his benefit. This required that he understand cause and effect. Later, we then have megaliths and social order of a ritual nature requiring him to understand the concept of organization on a higher level- this required more advanced vocal capabilities and deeper thinking.

The advent of writing is important within the occult also- the earliest writings we see are almost invariably of two types; those used for commercial purposes and those used for spiritual purposes. In the former case we have clay tablets all around the world of antiquity inscribed, for example, with the contents of urns and number of urns present during a trade- a quite sophisticated form of credit system or something of that nature. This seems to have been common in Rome.

OCCULT PHILOSOPHY

In the latter case we have all manner of inscriptions as well- Sumerian clay tablets contain everything from musical notes (which have been partly transcribed) to incantations.

But it is in the period of enlightenment, or shortly before, that one of the most important of all occult discoveries was made. The Rosetta Stone, found by the French under Napoleon in Egypt during his various excursions into North Africa and the Middle East. The Rosetta Stone, above almost all other discoveries within archaeology, has opened the door to the ancient, because without it we might know little or nothing about Egyptian Hieroglyphics. While this does not complete our knowledge of the language used, it fills in most of the gaps that were present at the time and opened up a vast store of knowledge for translation, which is ongoing still to this day on the power of the sheer number of remains in the region.

We see this very Napoleonic campaign referred to in the *Black Pullet* whose author is still unknown. While the talismanic arts referred to therein seem to be more metaphoric than literal there is still a deeply spiritual energy behind its authorship, and it isn't unthinkable that an actual soldier serving in Egypt at the time wrote it- in fact it isn't unthinkable that this individual *did* meet some Turkish mage in the shadow of the pyramids. We do know that the work dates to this time period, at least, since extant early copies have survived in the original French.

Human culture operates on cycles not remotely unlike celestial movements. Beliefs are invented, rise, stagnate, and die over time, as man's subjective understanding changes in accordance with cultural evolution- little of what we understand to be true will be understood as such in a few centuries and little of what the ancients believed is still believed in. Some of this is lunacy and shows mans inconstant nature and constant ambitious desire to improve even what has already been perfected, but some of it is desirable and works well for his physical purposes.

OCCULT PHILOSOPHY

The occult is forced to reject some of this change in accordance with its own understanding of the world, but the occult, too, changes with time. The types of elaborate ceremonies practiced in antiquity are now uncommon and have been replaced by more simplified workings, and in the current era, as of this present time, even the more simplified ritualism is being replaced by the rise of the modern occultist, which has forsaken physical books in favor of the vast libraries of the digital world, and who has forsaken nature for the urban enclave. This roughly mimics paranormal research as well, for we have stopped looking for dragons in the mountains and now begun to look for ghosts in abandoned industrial structures.

However, here there is further wisdom to be gleaned; the modern move towards the technological and urban has had a biting backlash against the same movements within the occult, Pastoral naturism and appreciation for pagan lore has now also seen a resurgence, and it has split the occult apart, because some are moving steadily towards a vaguely secularized understanding of magick, and others are adopting practices that are even more ancient and natural than the Victorian magick which had been common for so long. In other cases there is a fusion of these two (which I view as positive although this is opinion only.) In these cases, modern technology and nature go hand in hand in magickal experimentation. When I realized there was a digitized Ouija board on the internet I had a good laugh, then quickly realized that people were also buying actual Ouija boards at an accelerated pace, convinced they had occult value. I am not sure that the average demon is willing to possess a board game for the amusement of the casual dabbler in the black arts, but it's a good show nonetheless.

OCCULT PHILOSOPHY

Human culture and its understanding of the world moves in two cycles- there is the sub-cycle and the super-cycle, as we may term them.

The super-cycle is the rise and fall of long ages of mankind- we think of, for example, the Medieval era, or the Renaissance, or the Industrial era. The sub-cycle is shorter- and with the rise of technology roughly in the wake of the industrial revolution of the 1800s the sub-cycle has become as important as the larger super-cycle, since advances are now being made more quickly. It is on this bifold basis that the ages advance.

For example, let us consider the iron age and the rise of Rome. Rome typified the entire age, but within that long expanse there were multiple subsets of Roman culture. Its first incarnation was similar to its Greek predecessor- for it was composed at the political level by a legislative body of Praetorians, and was what would then be considered a fairly open, tolerant society. Immigration filled the entire Italian peninsula as Rome expanded, eventually crushing Carthage and consolidating its power. At this time, it was not technologically that much more advanced than some of the other surrounding cultures, and thrived mainly because of a combination of its superior capability to assimilate talented outsiders, coupled with its strategist consuls.

Then Rome faced northern barbarians and feared for its own existence as a large nation (for it was not truly yet an empire)- it then moved to a second era marked by imperialism, expansion for expansion's sake- egotism amongst its ever more powerful leaders. As Julius was killed the age of Caesars began and Rome became a more closed, intolerant society, yet one which continued to grow nonetheless on the power of military reforms and the rapid increase of technology. Crude leather vests were replaced by jointed iron armor which was so advanced that even a modern bolt will not penetrate it. They designed weapons of a horrifically advanced nature which would have overrun anything that existed from the fall of Rome and antiquity all the way to the middle of the Renaissance.

OCCULT PHILOSOPHY

The final age was one of stagnation- Rome eventually realized that its largely maritime movement of goods (for land trade was still inefficient) was unable to cope with its vastly expanded northern possessions and one by one they were overrun. Eventually, Rome itself was sacked by Alaric and the illusion of invincibility which had been their final cultural refuge fell. In time, Rome shrank to half its former size, and this Byzantine Eastern hold also eventually sank into darkness, specifically because its technological progress was slower than the Ottomans and other groups which supplanted it.

It took many centuries for Rome, as with other antiquated cultures, to cycle through even these shorter cycles- and the super-cycle involved stretched from shortly after its founding as a culture (which quickly became a regional power) all the way to the fall of Rome itself- a period of roughly 1,000 years.

Each successive era is shorter than this. When Rome was sacked the subsequent dark ages did not last quite one thousand years before the Renaissance began to peer up like a glowing sun over the horizon, casting aside the shadow of the misery which had lasted from shortly after the first sacking of Rome to the birth of the age of exploration. Subsequent to this, as exploration began in the new world, it was only a matter of a few centuries before this was in turn also supplanted by the era of revolution. The era of revolution was then supplanted in turn only a century later by industry. Industry was supplanted less than a century later by the world wars and the era of alienation and confusion. This relatively short, not even half-century super-cycle ended the moment atomic weapons were developed. This cold war lasted also less than half a century, and modernity (or more appropriately the age of globalism) began.

In the last two decades we have slowly shifted out of this subsequent age as technology has led from enforced globalism to voluntary globalism, with the former encountering increasing resistance on all sides. In fact, we are cycling back towards an era of national consciousness and the rediscovery of the past. Even modern music is a throwback.

OCCULT PHILOSOPHY

Now we have to consider the eras of occultism, for they overlap seamlessly with these eras.

Starting with Rome; as Rome is founded and begins to grow so too does its spirituality- it is pantheistic and legalistic. Over time Rome *forsakes* its tolerance for foreign people, but *adopts* tolerance for outside spiritual forces. Most barbarian gods found their way into the pantheon over time, and were subsequently legalized. Their rituals follow the same format- for many even venerated the emperor, or former emperors, as deities.

As Rome fell and the dark ages began occultism too fell into a dark age. Since the Romans had christianized, they persecuted all the spiritual forces they had formerly embraced. The occult, then, was found in two forms in this era; first in the form of christian mysticism, and second in the form of heretical underground mysticism (or that which existed outside of the christian-controlled corpus of Europe.)

As the Renaissance began science and the occult began to co-develop. Both were suppressed. As the era continued, though, this suppression became less prevalent, since some of these scientists and occultists were also working with monarchs and developing weapons or other innovations which made them immune to persecution. Here, occultism was veiled by science and intertwined with it. The core of what would become revolutionary-era philosophy begins here as aberrant notations on celestial bodies and the nature of hierarchies.

As the era of revolution began the occult began to rediscover a great deal of lost lore; not only because colonial militaries had moved into the ruins of antiquity and begun to dig up relics, but also because Greek and Roman pagan culture directly affected the philosophies of the same revolutionary groups cropping up in France and the United States, as well as elsewhere. The United States even has its own metaphoric pagan goddess; Columbia, alluded to in various satire and poems also from this era. This goddess now exists as a real thought form and watches over our nation, although very few people realize it.

OCCULT PHILOSOPHY

The industrial era was also of great importance. For the first time the world saw true urbanization and began to leave behind the long eras of wanting and entered the happy times of having. This spawned extremely egotistical, often materialistic occultism, and many such works exist. From this era we get numerous folk magick spells in both Europe and the Americas which deal with securing marital fortune, wealth, and so forth- the last time these had been prevalent seems to be in the golden ages of antiquity when industrialization already existed on a smaller scale (Rome, as a city, was technically industrialized, with standardization of measurements and crafting, organized mills, aqueducts, and so forth.) In fact, we might say the mid 1800s was very much like the 100s.

As this passed into the era of world struggle and confusion we get the first rudiments of "modern" occultism. This Edwardian period coincides with the mixture of magick with photography, music, and other artistic and expressive mediums. A large number of photographs depicting real or fictitious (mockup) ritualism survive from the period- there was an element of paganism in it as well, and sexual ritualism was intertwined with the more pragmatic pornography of the era also.

The moment that the Manhattan Project yielded its final results the world moved into an era of bipolar paranoia and stalemate-driven political and social maneuvering. The East became rabidly atheistic and the West rabidly religious in the organized sense. Everyone worried, that any day they would be vaporized. The music became louder and more frantic, more confused and insane- so too did the occult. At this time cults were spawning faster than they can be documented. Psychotropics are rediscovered and hippie shamanism and new agery combined with the darkest ritual occultism in melting pot cities like San Francisco. We might regard Woodstock as a gigantic (and successful) ritual to bring peace, wherein over a hundred thousand drug addled hippies held paganistic orgies and screamed to Gaia and Gandalf to save them from "the bomb." The fact that it seems to have worked is obvious, since not long after support for war seems to have utterly crumbled in the world and the first truly fruitful SALT talks began.

OCCULT PHILOSOPHY

The end of this era, as the Soviet Union was crushed by severe economic pressure and social restructuring, coincides with the rise of what we consider modernity; however in a century our era will be considered antiquated also, so this term should be avoided. In reality, we were, in the late 1980s and into the 1990s, in a very short period where nobody really seems to have known what to do. It seemed like there were no more foes to conquer and no more wars to wage, and so society turned inwards. It was at this time, let us remember, that the Satanic Panic emerged, and atheistic but ritualistic orders, as well as various pagans and Wiccans, were persecuted by christians at this time almost as badly as they had been in the burning times. Occultism was driven back underground and largely disappeared for a time.

And so now we come back to the present era, which began around the time televangelism began to die, roughly in the ending days of the 1990s as the internet arose as a dynamic force. Now, occultism is reaping the rewards and organized religion, for the first time since the age of revolution, has experienced a mass setback. Attendance and religiosity are being crushed under the electrified foot of the world wide web, and cults and orders of tiny sizes are now finding new ground. Every ancient text is now available for anyone to read, often in multiple languages. Newer occultists can easily and seamlessly publish any material they wish to create, in video form, audio form, or in text- they can conference with other occultists on the other side of the world.

It is in this condition that we now find ourselves; the occult has returned and technology is at the fore of its new-found capabilities, *but* it is also causing more physical ritualism, and physical organization at the more local level, to be suppressed. The backlash as I stated, being that such orders are also growing as occultists growing tired of isolation filter in, tentatively feeling their way into various groups they feel fitting for their own belief systems.

OCCULT PHILOSOPHY

THE CYCLE OF PHILOSOPHY

In the same way that all other matter, energy, and form oscillates and cycles, so too do man's philosophies- for this is a natural facet of existence and the natural state of reality.

So often, we regard reality as static and thus regard our understanding of it as subjective- but, here, perhaps there is another meaning behind this; perhaps reality itself is subjective and our understanding malleable because reality is malleable. Surely, to the occult, this is the case, because the occultist often seeks to alter or mold reality. So too does the shaman, with mind-warping substances.

The cycle at work here is that philosophy moves the same way spiritual forces or cultural ones do- just as a nation may be born, grow, die, and revive later, so too may a philosophy do so. We have forsaken many older philosophical schools and later revived them in new form under new names. This is the case with Stoicism and Epicureanism especially; both were destroyed and revived over and over. The Stoic philosophies of some antiquated cultures later revived in the dark ages when the philosophy of "put your nose to the grindstone and hope it gets better" was essentially all people had to survive. Survivalist philosophy always seems to be prevalent when times are hard. When times are better hedonism becomes preferable, as we see with the revival of what may loosely be termed Epicurean beliefs in the modern age paired with more ecstatic hedonism on the part of some.

Just as there is a natural rise and fall within a nation's economy (boom and bust being the oversimplified term for this phenomenon) there is a rise and fall between the oscillating schools of hedonistic philosophy and stoic philosophy- there are many smaller schools within them, but here we can differentiate between two primary schools; those which are ascetic or concerned with the withholding of materialism or the renunciation of carnal things, and those which are concerned with liberty and celebrating the carnal, or else promoting physical wealth and enjoyment in some way.

OCCULT PHILOSOPHY

As we speak currently the world is in the latter part of this oscillation. Most of the world, today, is developed to the point where even the poor are able to enjoy life insofar as they are capable of working, and although our economic structure is woefully uneven and gives reward mostly to those which do no work at all (read; those with enormous wealth who merely invest and manipulate it) most of those on lower rungs have what they need and at least some of what they desire. Oddly, we could as a culture restructure this and maintain massive wealth and upward mobility and pure capitalism while at the same time spreading that topmost tier's wealth around, in recognition of the fact that it benefits nobody and is primarily an oligarchic and corporatist enslavement of the majority of the economy by the *truly* wealthy. Anybody who believes a surgeon is rich has no idea what they're talking about- it takes them a year to make as much as some banking barons and oligarchic corporatists make in a day. It's not even really capitalism, but this is a peripheral subject at best and need not be expounded upon further here.

Epicureanism is, in essence, my philosophy of choice- for it is hedonistic in declaring enjoyment and happiness to be good, but also stresses that achieving this enjoyment requires, in many cases, living simply and learning to enjoy things that to not require extravagant wealth. Physical endeavors which bring wealth can also be enjoyed. I enjoy writing; it can result in wealth, and it will always, for me, result in happiness. Gardening is enjoyable; it yields healthy food at a low cost, requiring only that the gardener enjoy themselves, assuming they find amusement in doing so. The Epicurean school is, to my mind, superior to all others, although it would scarcely be possible to employ its philosophy under a tyrannical regime.

As times grow more difficult some of this hedonism will naturally be cast aside and be replaced by a more stoic philosophy, simply because those who have such philosophies to begin with, or begin to adopt them, will succeed, and those with a more hedonistic outlook will necessarily suffer as they realize it is less easy to acquire the means to enjoy themselves- specifically because *their source of enjoyment is corrupted.*

OCCULT PHILOSOPHY

Let the occultist now consider this; if a person's enjoyment comes from extravagant things- from expensive cars, mansions, gold and silver and gems, and all the facets of massive worldly wealth, he or she will very likely end up miserable. All of these things, in time, will decay, and it could be that in their very lifetime, a cataclysm or era of misery of some sort will replace the splendid order of hedonism we currently enjoy, and that they will find these things worthless, or at least worth less. In this case, they will find themselves parting with all of that wealth, selling it off to those who still manage to produce, in order just to survive.

The most recent period of wealth, post depression, that the west has enjoyed should be seen as aberrant, not normal- through most of human history we have never seen such a period, and there are things ahead for us that are likely to cripple our own wealthy order. Those with massive fortunes needn't worry because they control the political system and thus have the protection of various officials and armed police and soldiers, but the average person is likely to find their job further mechanized in the future, reducing the need for their own manpower.

The true way of hedonistic enjoyment is not therefore in worrying about wealth as a direct source of enjoyment, but rather a means to purchase other things that are enjoyable- if those things are productive and thus the manner of enjoyment productive, this individual has a far greater chance at success than someone who squanders the wealth away for a sports car that they won't be able to buy gas for the next time a depression comes around (and it will, eventually, for all things must pass.)

The wise occultist already derives immense pleasure from certain productive endeavors- the academic regardless of the field, or from nature, or crafts thereof derived from nature, or from being in solitude in nature, or from raising crops or from music or art, or perhaps something else along these lines.

OCCULT PHILOSOPHY

Eventually, in time, another period of abject misery will strike. Man will fall into darkness, but those who understand these concepts won't be particularly concerned; for them less will change, because they already enjoy things which do not require, say, electricity or vehicles. To them, the world is already very much like that which for all others it is likely to approach upon this encroaching era of misery and want.

However, in time, this too will pass; the age of involuntary stoicism will die and wealth will return, gushing forth from mines and farms and factories, and people will immediately delude themselves once more into thinking it will last forever, for the human has an aberrant belief in the permanence of the manner of living. So, too, does this cause nostalgia, amongst those who remember the world as being very different (and usually they dishonestly claim, better) "when I was a child" or "when I was younger." This is mostly delusional and the world was more or less the same in their youth.

The occultist, in their wisdom, should reject this oscillation and apply themselves to merely the natural order- the misery of the masses in times of want results often from their embracing of materialism for materialism's sake- there is no natural, logical reason why their gigantic homes and fast cars bring happiness, and in fact they bring misery, because it becomes necessary for them to continuously spend yet more wealth on them- wealth that at no time is guaranteed, unless they are in that very happy class with a choke-hold on the world economy. The richest nation can suddenly fall from its height into depression, destroying most of the material wealth of the entire economy (often a depression caused by the manipulation of the very same wealth holders, for spite or from misbegotten dealings.) The natural order is the enjoyment of the natural- this is the school of the occultist ever dwelling in the springtime of their spiritual development, and they are likely to find the materialistic world rather strange. Other practitioners of the magickal arts, who have fallen into the same trap as most people in the world, will scarcely be happier than the rest in such a time of collapse, and will likely apply "magick so called" to try and retain wealth- their endeavors will be mostly fruitless.

OCCULT PHILOSOPHY

If we were to draw out an exceedingly long time line in human development we could find eras in which culture and philosophy overlap in such a way that both are quite positive, and eras in which they are both quite negative. In other times they are mixed, and only one is positive and the other negative.

In the middle of the dark ages we see both cultural and philosophical upheaval- thus the center of the medieval period is remembered as the time of greatest suffering in recorded history- the political leaders of the day were despots, the religious leaders lacked wisdom and applied themselves to abuse and usury, the economies of most nations were small or nonexistent, and the philosophy used by the masses was one of abject misery as well; they sought wealth but had none, and thus suffered all the more. The church, in a moment of dim spiritual awakening, realized this and attempted to get rid of the gambling, drunks, and prostitutes in order to improve the social order, without improving any other aspect of life- as such instead of being received well as an attempt to improve the philosophy of the masses it was seen as just yet another abuse laden onto the backs of the poor by the church- for the rich merchants and monarchs continued in their extravagance and the wedge between leader and people was ever larger, with the church immune from all threats because no monarch dared oppose the decree of the same.

In some parts and areas of the dark ages this social order saw a host of reforms; Charlemagne, for all of his despotism on the battlefield, *was* a reformer, and actually knew how to read and write- quite an accomplishment for a monarch in his age when most leaders were more concerned with collecting treasure than ruling by reason. At this time the first academies and concerted efforts at building trade began to creep back after their collapse when Rome was burned by Alaric.

However it is not until much later in the end of the high middle ages and the birth of the Renaissance that things begin to improve very much- the plague killed so many people that fallow and free land was lying about for the taking by anyone willing to work it, and seed was free as well from the fallow plots of lords who had died.

OCCULT PHILOSOPHY

This coincides with one of the best eras; the Renaissance retained a lot of the poverty of the middle ages but the level thereof was reduced and the people had more of a chance to attain marginal wealth. Most of Europe had eaten nothing but bread and beer for centuries, and now they found themselves enjoying vegetables and fruits and wine as well, along with meat, which had formerly been hoarded by the rich and was well outside of the budget of the feudal peasants.

At the same time everything was reformed except for the church, which actually became more despotic than ever- but the church also lost a great deal of social sway as people observed that throughout the time of the black death the priests had alleviated exactly none of their suffering and had fled from the miasmas like cowards, hiding in their churches, walling up the entrances and praying to be spared instead of praying for the already dead. Small wonder the flagellants gained such popularity- even if their extreme actions failed to stop the pestilence they at least made an attempt and were available for the public to speak with. The age of the iron fist of the pope had ended, and all the church could now do was continue to unleash its tormenting devils- its inquisitors- on remote populations to keep them enslaved.

However the best era of all was the birth of the revolutionary era- the amount of liberty spread across the world, however brief it lasted, for the first time saw the rise of a population in which even the very poor would become literate and even those employed at mediocre ends would attain some level of wealth and stability. We have fallen astray from our actual founding goals, in the west, but this is redeemable and likely to change, and perhaps we will be lucky and this new era of wealth and liberty will happen during our own lifetimes- it would be remiss not to note that there are occultists out there in the world actively using their means to spread freedom into even the most despotic dictatorships. I can think of a few Saudi Arabians I myself have spoken with who are getting very tired indeed of the theocracy there, and more than a few westerners have begun to abandon the jaded, dying parties which exist here. We say, *Ave Columbia* and praise be to liberty- for a free people are an occult people.

OCCULT PHILOSOPHY

THE CYCLE OF CULTURE

Cultures, as well, cycle and change over time.

This goes hand in hand with philosophy but it goes beyond it- the sense of the people towards the world around them, and that which is considered desirable or undesirable, fluctuates in the span of a nations' existence regardless of the philosophy applied to the nation at large- in both cases (culture and philosophy) we speak in terms of a generalized *whole* although individuals within the nation or culture will not necessarily belong to the same system or school of thought. We might find a few stoics in the most hedonistic society or a few hedonists in the most stoic, just as even the most liberalized culture contains moralists and visa versa.

The west is currently moving into what would be loosely classed as liberalism, although there is a strong and growing undercurrent which is skeptical of both traditional leftist and right wing politics and cultural modes and is disdainful of both, preferring simply the line of "leave me alone, and I will leave you alone."

The east, however, especially in Russia, is moving in the opposite direction; hard times and political change there have led to the adoption of moralism and conservatism in a cultural sense while retaining the interventionist policies of the past. That this is a recipe for disaster in the east is clear, but what isn't clear is whether this is happening primarily due to charismatic top-down pressure or whether it's the result of the masses being misled into adopting such beliefs and then tolerating them at a doctrinal level. I will say little else about politics in a direct sense here since they are such an artifice, but we do have to mention the interaction between the west and east nonetheless because the two pose as moral opposites; the sides have, amusingly, changed almost entirely.

OCCULT PHILOSOPHY

In the world today there are two major polar powers which influence all neutral parties, and the occult is definitively behind both of them, in the post world war two period, we will have to cover here a small amount of history, some of which is rarely discussed.

During the second world war both the communist east and capitalist west marveled at how a formerly weak Germany managed to so swiftly rectify its ailing economy and restore mass order- National Socialism, regardless of the ills ascribed to it, turned out to be monumentally effective in crafting a volkische social system and a thriving economy; rapid technological expansion was so close to the new modern pace that we might say that, for some as-yet unknown reason, the Nazi party was advancing faster than any of their foes.

Within the occult this is understood primarily by noting that the entire Germanic center of Europe had decided to indulge in Atlantean lore and thus felt it had a national purpose, at a time when most of the world was losing its sense of national consciousness- the world had just barely exited from the anarchist Dadaist period of art, and from the first rudiments of the influence of music and occultism which came not from "white" and "western" circles but from elsewhere. The National Socialists seemed not to care, and instead of relegating these systems to second class status Himmler himself led expeditions into Tibet, Nepal, Egypt, and elsewhere, and sent archaeologists, linguists, and scientists into every desert, jungle, and mountain range he could find funding for, returning to his all-too-obviously occultized *Wewelsberg* to pour over books and manuscripts and to order translation and copying thereof. While Himmler was best known as a chicken farmer (and one of a strange nature beyond even his Atlantean obsession) none can deny that the sort of fringe materials he and others studied led to the embracing of pseudoscience which led to at least a few technological advances. One look at the prototyped flying wing will tell the sane observer that the Nazis weren't afraid to bend convention, even if we regard their culture itself as having been rigorously opposed to what we see as modernity.

OCCULT PHILOSOPHY

In this strange condition the Nazis fell and the Russians and Americans and British poured in and swiftly adopted every Nazi scientist and doctor they could round up, giving them residency and employing them in everything from burgeoning space programs to military contracting firms. In the United States this was termed *Operation Paperclip* and it's no small feat for the west to go from flying biplanes to going into orbit in only two decades. Amusingly, the same Nazis the United States once sought after to kill were now at the head of organizations responsible for so many technological advances in ballistics, aviation, electronics, and agriculture, that we might say the entire cold war era was marked by the west embracing the occultism of the Nazi party; for the occult studies performed were direct precursors and guides to their technological leaps and bounds. This is rarely spoken of specifically because of the conspiratorial nature of the subject. Russia, too, adopted such scientists, although they preferred threatening to kill their families should they not work hard enough.

In this cold war era the bipolar world of the USA and USSR formed; and the two cultures and their spirituality both grew to become polar opposites. In the early days the USSR was strictly atheistic and extraordinarily interventionist. The West (the USA and its close allies) became thus very pious and spiritual, and adopted extreme laissez faire and free trade systems designed to out compete the USSR and its sphere. This tactic worked, and decades later the east imploded utterly.

In the modern era, though, it is now *Russia*- the frozen center of that same old USSR, that is moving into the realm of social and spiritual piety and moralism, and the United States, now, is moving into secularity. Here we see the nearly complete oscillation of the cultures of the two polar powers. However, the spiritual cycle is moving more quickly than the cultural, for Russia retains its interventionism and the West has barely adopted any, and remains more or less concerned with free trade and a laissez-faire economic model.

OCCULT PHILOSOPHY

In this regard alone we see the disconnect between spiritual philosophy and actual culture; they are entirely separate cycles which affect one another without relying upon one another directly. The fact that the east is becoming morally authoritarian while retaining fiscal interventionism is a disaster waiting to happen, and the results can only be negative; isolation and stagnation may set in, or a new nuclear race might begin, or they might become even more draconian and end up with rampant destabilization.

The west is not much better off, to be sure- what little interventionism has been adopted has dumbed down our standing in the world and decreased our impact in foreign areas where we once had the free cash to edge in on. Most of our key allies have followed this same movement towards anti-spirituality as well, for Europe is even more secular than the United States is these days.

Even the types of employment considered important have changed. In the west we briefly stopped considering the carpenter, machinist, or mason as important, although this is now reversing. For a time we considered that our children were only worthy of praise if they got a degree and became an academic; even though those fields quickly became exhausted and many of them ended up out of work. "At least they went to college" seems to be the modern ethos, even if they are working alongside middle school dropouts and competing for the same low wage work.

In the east praise and adulation for the working peasant- the farmer or the career lowbrow soldier or the baker- has been replaced by the same fervor for ambition that the west had recently adopted; the Russian now wants to become a businessman or a professor, even though this will necessarily lead to the same overloading of the same fields we have just ourselves suffered through. Such is the folly of those who have not studied history.

OCCULT PHILOSOPHY

Importantly, and here the main point; the type of occultism coming out of these two poles has changed also.

Read the type of occult works indicative of the middle cold war period, those made in the United States or most of Europe; you will find that much of its is concerned with reincarnation and astrology and crystals and things of this nature. People were so paranoid about nuclear war that the only thing on their mind was how to escape the finality of death. They wanted to believe there was something beyond- something enjoyable- and the church had fallen short of delivering it. The pious preacher on Sunday reverted to the chain smoking drunk on Monday, and half his congregation went home and cracked open a work on the yogic system or how to curse your enemies.

Now look at the type of modern occult texts which are made here in the west- there is less of a focus on such things, philosophy has become more introspective and in some cases occultism more materialistic, or more concerned with technology (the Ouija board and other material objects of a supposedly arcane nature.) This has resulted from the lack of fear of imminent death that so marked the period prior to the collapse of the USSR, and has been affected by, and in turn affected, culture.

Now look to the east- the secular and folklore style recordings of spirituality within their academic circles which had been documenting the occult as though it were mostly a field of educational study have been replaced by actual hands-on guides to everything from the healing of herbalism to treatises on black magick- I have spoken with those from formerly soviet controlled regions and they attest to this- there is a definitive uprising as we speak in the Balkans, Russia, and elsewhere, focused only on the most dark aspects of the occult arts- especially with a focus on actual, physical sacrifice, which might be seen as connected to that ever present vein of economic misery present there. The quasi-ritualistic killings of the Dnepropetrovsk maniacs in Ukraine attest to the lack of care for human life found in some of these ritualistic workings, although only a few occultists have noted the seemingly ritualized aspect of these specific events.

OCCULT PHILOSOPHY

OCCULT PHILOSOPHY

THE CYCLE OF SPIRITUALITY

It is known within the occult that time moves upon cycles; it is neither linear nor strictly cyclical, with each interlocking mechanism therein, whether anthropic or celestial, affecting the likelihood of various spiritual outcomes.

Time is actually composed of a series (perhaps infinite) of interlocking gears and lines, which affect one another the way cellular machinery affects the composition, contents, and functions of a cell; rather than think of it as a simplistic line or circle, we must begin to think about it as a more complex mechanism composed of parts which cause one another to oscillate, cycle, and change course in unpredictable patterns, wherein only the smaller movements are predictable. A star may shine for billions of years, with its planets in orbit around it for spans of time we consider almost incomprehensibly large, but at the end of this very long predictable cycle, the entire system could be devoured by a black hole, ending it for billions of years more until the energy and matter is shot out in some other dimension, or spewed from the hole itself back into the universe at large- or perhaps it will stay there for what we could consider eternity, bubbling around in a compressed soup of atoms which no longer experience normal physical constraints.

We see this problem between the reality of time and our conception in the parable of 2012; many individuals were compelled to believe that the Mayan calendar, whose long count ended in that same year (technically the cycle did not complete until 2013 with the final *Haab* rotated back to its final position- this was ignored by doomsday conspiracists.) The west regards time as a line, and so everyone determined that the end of this count, and the apocalyptic revelations derived thereof, meant an end to time, or an end to the world, or some other final cataclysm- they imagined a pulse of matter from the center of the universe would expand outwards and doom us all or that Jesus would return. It was amusing to those who had studied the occult.

OCCULT PHILOSOPHY

In reality this system merely interlocks like gears and continues forever- there is no actual *end* in the sense we usually understand it. There are three major counts- the Haab and Baktuns being the most well known, and each Baktun, Haab, and other measure has its own meaning. This is an occult truth- you may be in a "bad" baktun but in a "good" haab and thus not suffer badly, or the baktun may be "good" and the haab "bad" and the same is the case- or both may be seen as negative, or as positive, and there are other counts as well. Tied into this is a super-count even longer than the baktun which wasn't even discovered until after 2012 had come and gone, and people chuckled and promised that they wouldn't believe such things again; but their failure to properly read the calendar stems from their inability to comprehend infinity and the interlocking manner of time.

The Mayans seem to have been about the wisest of those who attempted to quantify time- the west proclaims it to be a line, the east to be a circle, and some groups to be a sort of branching, spiraling fractal arrangement with little order holding it together; the Mayans alone seem to have understood it to be a complex (and perhaps infinitely complex) series of mechanical movements which can be represented literally as gears in ascending order, each affecting the others, each holding a different separate meaning.

The occultist can regard the movements of the sun and the moon and derive a great many illuminating conclusions from the same- but what occultist is regarding also the slow whirling of the universe as its own body, or of the galaxy, around whose central plane everything is rotating? Surely if the sun and moon are of occult importance, the larger composition of the entire galaxy is all that much more important- but I have met few people who regard it as such. This seems strange to me, like observing a pair of very small gears and ignoring the larger one affecting them both and being perturbed as well by both, for all celestial and anthropic things are constantly causing one another to perturb ever so slightly. Your own mass, when in proximity to another object, affects it, if only just a bit.

OCCULT PHILOSOPHY

Kali Yuga is an interesting concept as well; the Vedic cycle is normally measured in the many millions of years, although I have heard some secularize this concept and move it down to the hundreds or thousands (which also applies, indicating a finite mechanism easily broken down into smaller, similar cycles.)

Within the cycles of Vedic lore we have four main stages of existence.

First there is the *Satya Yuga* or golden age, in which virtue reigns supreme; all is spiritually aware and spiritually in tune. This is the most positive of the eras, but because there is peace, plenty, and prosperity, some claim that it is actually the most difficult age in which to attain true ascension, specifically because there are fewer obstacles to be overcome. It is difficult to amass good karma if there is no struggle present. I will here drag my own evolutionary theory into bearing; for as I said, it is the struggle which purifies, and in its absence, all is stagnation. So while this is the most outright positive, spiritual part of the cycle, it is also *the worst for those who seek enlightenment.*

The next age in declining order is *Treta Yuga* or the age of silver. This age contains mostly virtuous things, but also an element of materialism and corruption; nonetheless it is a desirable age for the spiritual, although more competition against obstacles is present. As such, it is slightly more difficult for a human to live a virtuous life than in the golden age, yet it is slightly easier to attain an ascended state as long as those obstacles are bypassed.

The third part is the *Dvapara Yuga.* This might be termed the age of bronze and contains about even parts good and evil. As before it becomes easier for a person to achieve an ascended state within this period because of the much greater obstacles to such success, but the number of people able to attain this state will decline.

OCCULT PHILOSOPHY

Kali Yuga is the lowest cycle here- for it is the age of iron. Hypocrisy, greed, and vice are everywhere, and human virtue is at its lowest possible point. Within Vedic lore these cycles last for great spans of time. What makes interpreting these four cyclical movements difficult is that different sects and schools which adapt the lore have changed the overall measure of the span involved- again, it can be over a million years in each movement, or even longer, or it may be boiled down to a few thousand or hundreds of years. We might here presume that the wanton materialism of the height of Rome right before its own vice collapsed it coincides with the last Kali Yuga, in which case we might regard ourselves as within the bronze, with the era of the Renaissance and enlightenment in between at the juncture of the golden age and the silver age.

If we use this modern standard of measure we can regard it either as the authentic system of Vedic lore with a smaller time measure as suggested by some, or we may regard it as a smaller cycle within the greater with the same meaning, for there are miniaturized oscillations within the Yuga system as well; the greater Yuga may be a million years in length, but surely there are smaller, lower gears performing much the same function for we can find no era of greed and hypocrisy that is without its virtues and no age of virtue without its faults. We might also apply it differently to different cultures, for perhaps they are separately governed (a concept Vedic scholars would likely dismiss as heretical.) In this smaller system I posit that the fall of Rome circa 410AD coincides with the end of the last Kali Yuga, and lasted until the early days of the middle ages around 710AD when the dark ages first began to wane tenuously. This bronze age then lasted until 1010AD when the silver age overtook it and the middle ages began. In 1410AD then, right at the dawn of the age of exploration, and the Renaissance began to peek over the horizon, the golden age began.

This golden age lasted into the enlightenment period of revolution circa 1810AD, and we are currently heading into the bronze age from the silver which would thus last until 2210AD. Each cycle thus in the smaller set lasts 400 years, or thereabouts. In 2610, we would thus enter Kali Yuga once more.

OCCULT PHILOSOPHY

Most Vedic scholars and others presume automatically that we are already in Kali Yuga because they look around and see nothing but evil; I do not personally believe this notion is necessarily correct; it is true that the world contains a great deal of vice, but this is being applied retrospectively to a system which did not predict the sorts of things we have in the modern age. We might say that especially in the period lasting from the Renaissance to the Revolutionary period, human culture was certainly in a sort of golden age- an age of expansion, with great amounts of introspection and occult wisdom flowing from every press and with the new literate middle classes absorbing educational material for the first time. Life spans increased, technology advanced, and yet man was still at the time mostly in harmony with nature.

We might also take the fantastic step of believing that man is in a golden age right now which changes the time periods involved on the basis of the rapid expansion of eastern thought and the concept of mutually assured destruction that regardless of its faults has prevented many a war- I reject this philosophically because the same weapons could at any time bring utter destruction to the world, and probably will in the future. For all the benefit of stalemate a great deal of destabilization is also present. As I write these very words, the doomsday clock is currently at three minutes to midnight- its most risky time reading since 1984 and one minute away from the level achieved during the Cuban Missile Crisis which very nearly destroyed the planet altogether. Surely had this happened any survivor remarking upon the occult would label it the cataclysmic end of an obvious Kali Yuga.

The important point here is that no Kali Yuga is the actual end of the world as understood by westerners; rather, it is merely the low aspect of a cycle. As a wheel turns, it completes its rotations, but the wheel does not magically stop existing or fall apart merely because it has completed such a rotation. Likewise, this turning may be regarded as appearing swift, the engine causing the motion is turning far more quickly, in a manner of convolution which forms a microcosm of existence.

OCCULT PHILOSOPHY

Here we have to warn against a slightly amusing aspect of occultism. Every time some self proclaimed prelate or high priest of darkness or new age "oracle" takes hold and begins to gain popularity, they seem to invariably do the same thing; declare that a new age of some sort has arrived, and the old passed away. This is normally accompanied by the waving of hands and the sounding of some ritual musical component along with a small group of hooded occult praetorians chanting "so mote it be" or "let it be so." If we believed all of these self appointed leaders and representatives of everything magickal we are now simultaneously in the age of fire, the new age of Aquarius, Kali Yuga, a golden age, Ragnarok, the age of the coming of Jesus Christ, the age of the coming of the Mahdi, and the age where the green ants will wake up and destroy the world because of uranium mining in the outback.

Surely all of these ages don't actually coincide for the totality of mankind- for that to be true the world would have to ascend, descend, be built anew, and be destroyed, all at the same time; unless we posit that all of these events merely describe the warping of our physical plane this cannot be the case, for the ages self contradict. We then have to find what corresponds, and what is sensible from a spiritual perspective, although we needn't exclude these sweeping declarations, but rather to relegate them to a more minor status. As I stated, no age of darkness is without virtue and no golden age without vice- the world may be ascending while one group or nation or tribe descends, or the reverse may be true and the world will plunge headlong into an aeon of fire and judgment while a few lucky groups avoid this because of their own spiritual capabilities.

Ragnarok, too, is misconstrued by the western audience. Certain pagans in Britain declared Ragnarok to have begun in February of 2014, but once again, as with the Mayan Calendar, westerners presumed this meant the world would be hit with a winter that would last several entire years during which time most of man would be destroyed, leaving only the metaphysical and sexual metaphor for the first couple, a term applied within each such cycle, rather than to specific individuals in a literal sense.

OCCULT PHILOSOPHY

In reality Ragnarok also refers to this cycling of the ages. Nowhere is it said that everything ends forever, other than the current age; we even see this in mythology understood to be fictional such as the works of Tolkein. The span of man's existence is measured in ages, with each one punctuated by some cataclysmic end or major social and cultural advance marking the procession of time; this does not mean that the world has been obliterated, merely that the old age as it stood has been altered in such a way that it is now antiquated. The eras referred to in paleontology, such as the Jurassic or Triassic periods, are much the same; each one lasts a given length of time, and ends because things have changed remarkably and the world is far different than it was in the age before. We look at, for example, that same Jurassic age, or the Cretaceous, and we see a wide variety of massive reptilian mega-fauna roaming the planet, and subsequent to the ending of the age of dinosaurs as the primary life form of note we end up with the age of mammals taking hold in which rodents amusingly have a better chance of survival than a thirty yard long Ultrasaurus which would dwarf any land dwelling creature in our world today. The age of the sauropods ended, but the age of life never ended at all- and even the most brutal of calamities would leave behind chemotrophic life forms, radiotrophs, and various photosynthetic and fungal life forms, or at least most likely would do so.

Organic molecules can last for millions of years on an asteroid hurtling through space- organic life will not stop existing on our planet regardless of the kind of misfortune it may experience, and here is the truth as well of Ragnarok- a two year winter would cripple mankind and destroy a large proportion of advanced species on the planet but there would remain others, and man too would likely remain if only in scattered pockets where they possessed the means to outlast the cold. The metaphor of Ragnarok is merely a metaphor for widespread destruction at the end of a given era, after which survivors once again recover and build a new world, which is not the same as before; a new age has been entered which will be markedly different than before.

OCCULT PHILOSOPHY

For one example we might use the dark ages. During this period most populations were illiterate, lifespans were short, and life was generally miserable and prone to sudden upheaval- despite this centuries-long misfortune man survived and emerged all that much more powerful after the age had ended. Also, antiquity remained alive in the form of remains left behind in ruins and temples all over what had been the Roman Empire, and as such western culture survived because the texts and inscriptions and artifacts of the past were still very much intact, to be rediscovered at a later date when man began rooting around in every pyramid and catacomb he could find roughly at the beginning of the era of enlightenment as colonial militaries moved into the desert to search for treasure. Ironic it is, that the real treasure they found was knowledge, much as the Templar had found in the middle east during their own excursions. Knowledge, not gold, was and always will be the greatest treasure of all. This is yet another occult truth- and you can be sure that any grimoire promising a pact with some spirit to find gold is actually steganographic in form and is trying to impart philosophical truth.

The I-Ching and Timewave Zero are also of interest within this subject although the former is more of a fortune telling system and the latter a modern day mathematical model which has been misused in multiple instances. According to the latter (based supposedly on calculating the former) there is a mathematical model and wave function which applies to human history and can be used to predict major events. Those seeking to retrospectively apply this to the Mayan Baktun movements manipulated both the function and the wave to make it seem like the wave ends and flat-lines in 2012, although it then merely expands back outwards when the original mathematics are used. Again, as before, this curve is not predicting an end of the world but merely the temporary hibernation of its own mathematical function at zero value, before it miraculously resurrects. Even the story of resurrection itself models this truth; it may be that the early christians who wrote about such things were attempting to craft a parable around this concept; that there is no "end" in the sense usually understood by a human, merely a period of sleep, or hibernation, or inactivity in some way before a return to physicality or to self awareness.

OCCULT PHILOSOPHY

Those who have used psychotropics understand this concept more than others- or at least this is my belief- after all it's fairly close to dying when you take certain substances in certain quantities, specifically some of the more potent hallucinogens like *salvia divinorum*. The DMT-derived concept of machine elves roughly mimics the creation process spoken of in the Bible, which seems irrelevant to occultism until you realize that both Atlantis-inspired new age groups and ancient ceremonial occultists considered sound important. I have spoken of the Hypogeum at Malta, and said that along with some other ancient sites it's probably the most occult location on the face of the Earth because of its own resonating chamber deep below where a pin dropping becomes audible many rooms to the side.

Some believe that sound was even used in the building of megaliths. It is true that modern science has developed the means to literally levitate small objects by broadcasting waves of sound over them within a three dimensional matrix- in this manner it is possible to move the object by causing it to "ride" two complimenting sound waves which resonate at the same frequency as the object itself. Nikola Tesla may be thought of not as just a scientist but perhaps the most important occult mind of the modern age, who said:

"My brain is only a receiver, in the Universe there is a core from which we obtain knowledge, strength and inspiration. I have not penetrated into the secrets of this core, but I know that it exists."

Tesla also appears to have been prophetic in nature- that being understood as having enough understanding to comprehend likely future scenarios. He also stated that it was not in the present that his findings would be considered important, but rather the future. This has come to pass in the present age, and much of what modern science is currently doing was either done first by, or spoken of first by, Tesla and a few other great minds in the same period. It is claimed he developed a weapon that could melt metals at great distances and cause seismic instability; this is likely, given his other musings on the nature of energy and vibration.

OCCULT PHILOSOPHY

Here we also see the more genuine nature of the occult. Most of the time people adopt a Hollywood-style view of magick and believe that the average practitioner of any sort of mystic art is a celebrity or at least a wealthy red-robed mage living in an old Victorian home and chanting from their top floor at the skies, while causing a mighty storm to roll in that floods surrounding areas, or they think of a black clad necromancer raising the dead and attempting to summon armies to do their bidding. In reality the more authentic occult is one of seclusion, which would not immediately be evident to outsiders- the occultist dwells in this state because the world holds little of value to their spiritual development; perhaps we are in Kali Yuga thus after all.

Even the Catholics believe in such things despite their abrahamic beliefs and their exceedingly organized approach- many believe that the higher tiers of the Roman Catholic clergy are aware of occult truths that the laypeople and basic monks and priests are not privy to; and this I believe may be one issue wherein the conspiracy-minded protestants are right, although they ascribe to it a wrong meaning. In their belief this is evidence that the pope and certain cardinals and peripheral orders (usually the Jesuits and/or Benedictines) as well as various Rosicrucians and Masons, are trying to take over the world, or else usher in the end at the hands of the antichrist which these same protestants imagine is the actual leader of the church. In reality this is evidence more that the Catholic church has decided to become guardian to ancient lore and to philosophical materials that either the world is not ready for or which they consider subversive. How strange that the same people claiming the Catholics are agents of Satan also claim that they possess a grimoire (called the true grand grimoire) which they have sealed off somewhere in the Vatican, and that this book is fireproof and obviously magickal yet the Catholics have steadily lost ground and never apparently made use of such a potent tome.

OCCULT PHILOSOPHY

It goes further; they have also a prophecy called the "prophecy of the popes" supposedly penned by Saint Malachy, although at least some of the entries there appear to have been penned later (for they are in an altogether different style.) Here I submit that Malachy was merely the author of the papal inscriptions therein which date to his lifetime and before, sort of a metaphor catalogue describing the popes themselves. Some unknown author added the rest on later, although there are a few uncanny similarities between the last few popes and their descriptions. According to this prophecy the world is on its last pope and the "terrible judge" is supposed to be here at any time. Time will indeed tell if their prophecy here is literal or not.

Even then, though, the Bible itself makes it clear that their own end times aren't a literal end either- the antichrist and assorted fallen angels are cast into a pit of fire and all of humanity appears to at last be spared (for the Bible never once makes the claim that sinners go into the same lake of fire as Satan does) and the world is renewed again. In this strange realm there is a city made out of solid gold as high as it is wide and long- literally forming a cubic structure- in which there are various strange and heavenly things such as trees which bear a dozen types of fruit and leaves which cure all illness and so forth. Taken as metaphor this reveals the heavenly state of the world in a future golden age after which some unknown agent of darkness has been purged. Taken literally it's still not a true apocalypse because the world returns to a living state and everyone therein is once again alive, in a very physical form at that.

We could speak also here about predictions made by any of a number of individuals- Dee perhaps, or Nostradamus. What ties these predictions together and makes them less accurate is that time is indeed not linear. In order for these predictions to be completely accurate (even if divinely or demonically inspired) we would have to posit a mechanistic cosmos, but the cosmos is not finite in this manner. As such, predictions can be made which will be more accurate than others upon recognition of *parts* of the mechanism but they can never be wholly accurate.

OCCULT PHILOSOPHY

Further though, we have to recognize that most such prophetic materials regard only this planet and celestial phenomena observable from our planet- as such the number of mechanisms required to be observed is a finite sum, because there is less of an affect upon the movements of humanity from great distances than from close ones, in the same way in which closely connected gears within a machine are more exactly affecting one another in a more finite, more easily predictable manner. For this reason we can say that fortune telling, prophecy, and similar divinatory arts are *potentially* accurate, but never potentially fully accurate. Then, also, there are charlatans and soothsayers which merely make good guesses, or get lucky, or who apply themselves to psychological sleight of hand and benefit nobody. These are more numerous than those which actually comprehend even the finite mechanisms of the universe.

There is also here the concept of generational spirituality which I will speak of for the first time, and it operates in a manner not unlike the Strauss-Howe generational theory (which is its own, secular concept.) Within that theory, there are four rotating archetypes of man; the prophet, nomad, hero, and artist, which coexist with four turning cycles of the same type; namely the high, awakening, unraveling, and crisis. These cycles each last twenty years (about the time of a generation) with the entire cycle lasting eighty years.

In this sense, we are currently in a crisis generation and those of my own age range children of the prior unraveling- Strauss and Howe would term thus this generation which I am a part of a hero generation, in which pragmatism and individuality reign. The subsequent generation, being born right now in the crisis period, will be happy to note that they will be happier, most likely, because they will come of age instead in a time of awakening after this crisis is over.

OCCULT PHILOSOPHY

This theory is based upon the conception of humanity as self-reactive. That is, that these four modes lead into one another as different generations come of age, and these generations naturally absorb the world around them in what Strauss and Howe imagine to be a more or less mechanical, homogenized manner. We can say only that the theory is true for a majority or plurality of individuals and cultures, not necessarily for all of them; a time of crisis in one nation is possibly a time of general peace in another, although even this interplay leads to the competition of these same cultures, where aggression between two lands or peoples is often preceded by misunderstandings of reality and culture itself. Spirituality moves in much the same manner.

The spiritual moves upon the same basis- generational cycles (which are not set in stone but are generally applicable) which last roughly the same amount of time as the cultural cycles spoken of prior; that is, that they tend to overlap, because the cultural mode of a time period will necessarily influence the spirituality of the same generation, and that same spirituality will necessarily influence the following cycle as well, as different types of thought become popular or unpopular, lost or rediscovered. I posit that these two cycles overlap almost entirely.

We will here imagine four successive generations. First, a period of general spiritual peace. We might think of this in terms of a period of religious and social tolerance, in which otherwise aberrant beliefs are tolerated insofar as they are doing no harm. Subsequently there is a period of revelation in which older spiritual systems become challenged and new ones posited. This leads to a third in which the old and new schools compete, driving a degradation of convention over this time span. In the final stage some of the old and new alike will be destroyed. This cycle then repeats on roughly the same scale as the Strauss-Howe and we are currently thus in the final part of this cycle, and fairly deep into it.

OCCULT PHILOSOPHY

We can see this modeled well in American history. When we think of the period of the late interwar and early cold war, the middle cold war, the end of the cold war and beginning of the new millennium, and finally the present era.

American spirituality in the late interwar and early cold war period was rudimentary and christian in form and had a sort of Andy Griffith style to it- the veneration of small town America, the idolization of the self made man, the lionization of your town pastor.

In the next period we see a massive host of new spiritual forms crop up- especially with regards to hippie spirituality and the anti-war period. Psychotropics enter the west en masse for the first time in modernity and help to spawn Satanism, modern Wicca, neopaganist revival, the resurgence of eastern spirituality, the introduction of the yogic system, the introduction of tantric spiritualism, and hedonistic nature worship. The old then spars with the new, as traditional christians are labeled "squares" and these new things "hip." This cycle involves music and art as well.

In the third period (beginning roughly at the end of the 1970s) there is a confused stagnation of all of these beliefs. They begin to attack and destroy one another where possible and every other film involves the occult. Fears of possession are everywhere, all is thrown into utter upheaval and people begin to adopt a near disdain of human life, reveling in the bizarre and fearful for their own sake, embracing the darker side of occultism which had been (partly) absent from the naturalism and anti-war sentiment of the prior period.

In the final movement, as crisis continues in the United States, the sudden increase of interconnected expression at the hands of the internet has begun to do what has never been done in a thousand years; religious christianity is dying as we speak and has been since the middle of the last period, and religious islam is currently experiencing its own throes. The left hand path is slowly subsuming the right.

OCCULT PHILOSOPHY

Finally here I will make a final notation, and it is intrinsic to understanding these cycles of spirituality- at the third and/or fourth stages of these cycles, a dying spiritual force may actually rapidly expand. Like an atomic explosion, this expansion is followed by a rapid dissipation of the energy involved and results in a lot of suffering and no lasting resolution. Christianity, in the mid and late 1980s, began to attempt to enforce its own doctrines and dogmas primarily by appealing to entertainment and became what it had previously attacked; a money-making endeavor and a corporate entity. This last gasp of christian zeal at first strengthened its hold on the population, but when the novelty of watching obvious charlatans rant in tongues and embezzle the checks of little old ladies wore off, these corporate entities mostly collapsed leading to a huge vacuum; people had been convinced it was okay to go to church by sitting in front of the television on Sunday as long as you sent your tithe to some minister in a studio in California, and so these couch potato christians, when deprived of their televangelism, simply gave up their religiosity instead of going back to the actual church when this era ended. As such, there are now thousands of abandoned churches and tens of thousands of empty churches awaiting sale across this nation, even though there are technically more christians- because few new christians are religious.

Islam is making the same mistake. In its embracing of technology, especially the internet, it is adopting the same materials it once so heavily criticized- technologies developed by what they imagine to be the great Satan of the west. As such, I predict that once their next awakening begins in a decade or so, islam will (in many areas) become a mere shell of itself, which will in turn lead to a future crisis as islamists begin to rediscover (using the same technology once shunned by islamic leaders nonetheless) old pagan forms from Arabia and Asia, as well as the joys of secularity. Time will tell if I am correct, but I already see it happening.

OCCULT PHILOSOPHY

EVOLUTION OPERATES ON NON-BIOLOGICAL PRINCIPLES

The process of evolution is normally seen in strictly secular terms; secular scientists embrace it as a genetic, biological process, and many religious individuals expunge it on the basis that it clashes with their conception of the world as divine- however these same individuals ignore the fact that the two may, and do, coexist.

Evolution as I stated is not to be seen, in an occult manner, as simply individual, discrete, competing life forms merely fighting over various resources and then changing over time in accordance with outside stimuli, but rather as diverged variants of the same primary original life form changing over time with those same stimuli in accordance with selective processes, which innately drive a form of temporary progress causing every possible niche to be filled- in this way these life forms improve one another but only within the short term, after which such improvements are necessarily re-refined over and over again. In this way, Lamarck and his own theories are *technically* correct but only within the very short span of time- in the longer span Darwin is closer to the truth.

In the short term, these divergent forms of the same original life are merely improving one another by competition. In the long term they are in some cases destroying one another or relegating one another to lower importance and population levels specifically because the process is weeding out what is weak, but here this process only acts this way within a stable system; the system is, however, unstable, and any advance may become detrimental if the system changes. Giraffes are a prime example- their necks have become longer over time because selection has favored it, but a prolonged period of famine in which their resources of choice decline would select instead for perhaps shorter necks, and the population would either change over time, or else suffer and perhaps die out altogether. In this way, extinction when driven by nature is not necessarily a bad thing and goes on all the time, and is merely the result of a weaker life form (weaker in a specific time period and system) being removed by one more suited for the same system and situation. This does not apply directly to artificial extinction driven by man, however.

OCCULT PHILOSOPHY

In the same way, religions evolve over time. Religions which oppose themselves to change tend to eventually experience a schism, in which some new sect branches from the original- almost invariably this is the result of a school within the original path embracing modernity to a greater degree and the larger religion itself shunning modernity and clinging to now outdated belief systems. The result is usually a weakening of the former, but at the same time, as with genetics and biology, the weaker original path may eventually strengthen again, either because it changes or the situation of the world changes. This is made more convoluted by the existence of many cultures and nations- we can see that the world has been partitioned into areas; the islamic world, the christian world, the atheistic world, and the generally tolerant multi-faith world specifically encompassing most of North America and Europe, as well as Australia and a few other cultures. So too are there cultures which have generally embraced Vedic religion or Buddhism.

We will here explain the evolution of religion by isolating any of these nations and cultures- take, for example, the United States. The culture of this nation has changed substantially in the last two decades, as the internet has gained dominance and smaller faiths have found themselves able to project their views to the wider world. So, too, are more secular beliefs for the first time experiencing a renaissance since the period of enlightenment when they first experienced the rudiments of tolerance from various western cultures. We see, then, that in this highly competitive reality, older fundamentalist paths are mostly dying off, and the paths experiencing this have begun to appeal to racialism and national identity to try and carve out an ever shrinking niche amongst the more radical tenets of the right hand path; this they do not out of actual strength but out of weakness, and most of these groups are losing favor to more "liberalized" christian groups. Meanwhile, secularism is exploding in size as too are ancient paths which are seen as more capable of coexisting with the cultural tolerance and environmentalism of our age.

OCCULT PHILOSOPHY

The concept of thesis-antithesis-synthesis does not seem to apply to this process as it does to the cultural cycle- in the case of religion it is more thesis-antithesis-competition-selective extinction. In this latter example the original religious order experiences a schism, and the two compete with one another and with outside forces. Eventually one side or the other is victorious and the other stagnates and begins to die off, and its members either embrace secularism or some other force, or join the victor in what is now seen as the "correct" path. This is perpetuated *ad nauseum* and is an ongoing process.

However, from time to time, especially when the original, stagnating group was very large (such as with Catholicism) the original group then experiences its own change and stabilizes, or else in some future era it finds its beliefs are once again part of the accepted and begins to grow again. Oddly, this can lead to the early gains of the schismatic group flagging off as the original school of religious philosophy once again overtakes it, and can lead to the newer group itself dying. In this way we might say that often what we're seeing is merely divergence of a few primordial groups which then improve one another much the same way I envision biological life forms doing, and that extinction is occasional rather than common. Unlike within biology, religious extinction is also reversible, since its beliefs can be written down and eventually rediscovered later. Hellenism, more or less dormant for a thousand years, has tens of thousands of actual, literal adherents now in the modern day, because its generally positive system is now being appreciated again as a religious force worthy of veneration by those who have chosen it out of many other forms of paganism, although Norse mythology has become the pagan form of choice outside of what may be seen as vaguely Americanized Wiccan pagan forms, which number in the many millions spread amongst several major schools, and including as secularism does an additional element of philosophy not aligned directly with an established order.

OCCULT PHILOSOPHY

This brings us to another important point; the interplay between spirituality, theism, and religiosity. I am myself spiritual, but I am also atheistic about most deities and rather agnostic towards the rest, regarding many as metaphor and symbol, or acknowledging them as indirect, distant deistic thought-forms. As to religion, I am almost virulently opposed to its very existence within established orders, which I see as corrupt. I am not alone in this path, within the occult.

It is possible for a religion to die altogether and its spiritual beliefs to be retained. It is also possible for the deity of a religion to be venerated directly or in a new form even after it original cult is decimated and forgotten. There are people in this world who venerate the great spirit of Native lore, who themselves know little to nothing about Shamanism or Mesoamerican spirituality. Some may term this "fluff" or say that it is inauthentic and thus negative or wrong; I claim rather that any form of such veneration is at least as likely to be "correct" as the original religious body, thus shunning the unfortunate element of purism some practice.

We must regard some religious orders as directly understood as well to have been fictional even by their founders; nowhere else is this easier to understand than with Mormonism, whose founder (and the author of their book) was a noted con man and criminal who finally got his due at the end of a rifle while attempting to flee the legal system. So too can we regard Scientology, which is a cult, understood to be a cult, and founded by a man whose own works prior to his apparent mental unhinging was strictly science fiction. We can quantify these two groups as fiction-based cults because they were spawned in relative modernity, although unfortunately it is more difficult to determine whether older religious groups were understood as such- at least some have claimed christianity falls into this same category, although the amount of extra canonical philosophical material from both Judaism and christian circles appears to indicate this is not entirely so.

OCCULT PHILOSOPHY

I previously spoke of islam dying out; this is true, although it may be more appropriate to merely say it is experiencing among the most dramatic and violent schisms we have seen in more than an age. We have to at least go back to the times of Luther to find a situation in which a religious group is changing so dramatically in such a short time.

In either case the situation is the same; a religion which refuses such a schism may in fact end up worse off than if it had allowed some of its more "modern" components to create a new branch or religion, because the entire faith will fall into infighting, which can become quite vicious. Even within christiandom as it stands currently, the two major branches present in the west- the Catholics and Protestants- fight with one another almost as much as they attempt to combat outside forces. Fighting on two fronts in this way is usually deleterious to the larger religious core, and here we see why they have largely failed to enforce their moralism on cultures and nations, because unless one finds itself mostly homogenous in a given area the two sides, despite both believing in Jesus, will proceed to hold decades-long debates on the nature thereof and get nowhere.

This is something the occult and the occultist ought to avoid. It is perfectly acceptable to criticize that which is unseemly and logically implausible, and it is fine to criticize the right hand path, but where criticism of other occult forms comes in, it ought to be more amicable disagreement than outright violent hatred of groups which merely comprise a different view of the ultimately same concepts. In this way, the occult will outpace the more organized, and usually obviously abhorrent, right hand path.

Likewise we might regard different schools of the occult, of magick, of naturalist spirituality and paganism, as merely different expressions of one singular, massive divine force or energy, or cosmic system.

OCCULT PHILOSOPHY

Technology additionally evolves in a manner similar to the principles behind biology; how can it be other than this, when technology is an adaptation employed by biological life forms? What is more effective within a given time period at solving some problem will be retained, what is less effective will be removed. Oddly, though, here we see a similarity to the religious schism and the rediscovery and re-use of older religious paths; for older technology is sometimes a trigger for nostalgia and begins to see new use, as is currently the case with vinyl albums which had been largely replaced by compact discs and later digital files altogether in the last few decades.

This principle- the evolution of technology- seems to lack any importance within the occult until we observe that the occult is co-reliant with technology. Where once a bookshelf stood, now there is a computer loaded with digital books, and where there was once a pipe organ there is now a synthesizer. The feel of the occult, over time, has thus changed as well. Again, as with technology itself, and as with the religious schism, the older style has returned once more as well- yet another cycle, for what is old can be appreciated again specifically because it is later seen as more authentic, or the mood it creates more conducive to ritualism.

In fact, everything in existence evolves according to the background it finds itself in- evolution is thus a series of cycles, with each convolution, each new level of complexity, being largely driven by mutagenic processes. It is the result of energy, often, that this is the case- literally radioactivity. Perhaps we can extrapolate this to the cultural and religious, for the energy a people finds itself enjoining in a given era- one of misery or one of happiness, one of wealth or one of want, will directly inform its decisions. The occult relies on this same basis. In a society without a concept of wealth, we would not expect to find a book containing charms and incantations designed to make the reader more wealthy, and if people had no finite life span they would not be concerned with spells designed for health increasing purposes.

OCCULT PHILOSOPHY

Things which are currently considered heretical will later become acceptable and things which are acceptable now will be regarded later as heresy. Because we are in a cultural cycle of upheaval despite our relative wealth we see this all around us- we are currently in an era in which it is considered unacceptable to regard race, for example, as important, and in which it is seen as acceptable (even laudable among some circles) to both support and partake in inter-racial marriage. If we were to enter a time machine and return to the 1950s, we'd find the opposite to be true; inter-racial marriage would be condemned by most and bigotry accepted and considered normal.

Both the cultural progressives and reactionaries look at this cycle and oscillation of human consciousness and regard it as good when the trend favors their own belief systems, and as bad when it doesn't. Likewise, both employ the media to proclaim that the other side, after so many such cycles back and forth as the wheel of time revolves, has died and will never again return to "plague" mankind- either with reactionary moralism and bigotry, or progressive lunacy and misplaced idealism.

Neither of these groups can ever be right because neither of them have grasped the concept that they're imaginary flip-sides of the same ever-rotating coin. It's the same coin, regardless of whether it lands on heads or tails, and there's nothing preventing the coin from being flipped over and over again. In fact, the progressives and reactionaries are their own worst enemy by using every means at their disposal to try and suppress the other "side" specifically because the people's consciousness will change regardless of how despotically they might cling to power, grinding down their critics. I claim this; that what progressives today call progress will be seen as regression in a coming era of moral reactionary sentiment, and that latter cycle, too, will pass by the wayside and eventually be seen as the dark ages by a future incarnation of western culture. Thus I say, both sides have valid points, invalid points, and are delusional and misled by virtue of not understanding the concept of eternal struggle and its manner of improving mankind.

OCCULT PHILOSOPHY

The occult can move in much the same manner. The sort of light workers and unicorns material of the 1980s taken, as it were, straight out of something by a young adult fantasy author, was the direct opposite to the rise of Satanism and similar veins of moral philosophy circa the 1960s and 70s. These two sides even fight today, even though they aren't sides beyond again being opposing faces on one coin. One side of the occult wants you to gaze into a crystal and chant with the celestial bodies, and the other side wants you to delve into the darkness of chaos and invoke some long lost demon.

The real struggle, then, and this is the further, purified occult truth in this passage, is simply struggle for struggle's sake, the eternal struggle or *kampf* so misused as it were in the past for political gain. It is not a cultural struggle, or a political struggle, or a struggle of the races; it is a struggle of everything, and every opposition, war, argument, debate, and disagreement man ever had has technically purified his being regardless of how monstrous we may perceive it as being.

There are of course misuses even of this process; a war may be started solely for fiscal reasons and this is quite often the case, but the individuals hurling themselves into such a gauntlet of madness will emerge more pure than they were before, having conquered fear of death and learned to desensitize themselves to its grasping hands. It is not always enough to become spiritually aware that death is an illusion (which it is) and must be carried further in some cases, to facing death itself in a literal manner without fear. Similar to war, class struggle and things of that nature are much the same. We see in Marx, for example, little else but inauthenticity and his entire system was predicated on a flawed understanding of anthropology- how sad it was, as communism spread out from its Marxist roots and devoured so many tens of millions of people. And how much more sad, that the average westerner knows of the holocaust but not the holomodor, specifically because it is now politically incorrect to compare these two similar events.

OCCULT PHILOSOPHY

EASTERN PHILOSOPHY IS WRONG

Eastern philosophy- here we speak about the general conception of time as quantified by the easterner- is wrong.

The eastern paths typically regard time as a circle- a circle being of course a finite line that merely intersects itself perfectly. In this conception, man occupies a nearly infinitely small, imaginary point on the circle, experiencing each such minute point at a time, and progressing through it. Thus, the east dimly comprehends the cyclical nature of time, while relegating it more or less to the finite, because this over-simplistic representation contains no interlocking gears, and is mostly static. They may represent time with several such circles interconnecting with one another and affecting one another within, say, a Yuga cycle, but even these larger movements, while seemingly vast, are finite as well.

This is pure nonsense and regards the cosmos as finite. Yes, they may in the modern age realize that it isn't, and is limitless, but they persist in terming the time cycle affecting man first and foremost as a circle- cultures, spiritual beliefs, and everything else is relegated to this finite system, leading to predictions which decay in usefulness as it repeats. Here the entropy is not in the cycle, but in the usefulness thereof in an occult, spiritual sense.

This has directly misinformed their notion of life itself. In the eastern paths you are born, live, die, and reincarnate. Some of these groups even see this as a bad thing and believe you should attempt to escape the process through severe asceticism. I ask this; is it truly a blissful notion, to become as nothing, and to stop experiencing the senses? I ask this only rhetorically because the answer is a resounding "no" unless life is absolutely filled with sheer misery. And if it is, then what- for in a future form you may not have such a miserable life. Moreover, the belief in this ascetic process is misused by the political heads, who realize their people are easily placated by meagerness of life so long as there isn't abject and total drudgery.

OCCULT PHILOSOPHY

The east has also grown hypocritical. The Dalai Lama proclaims to be reincarnated and enlightened, yet embraces Marxist economics which benefit nobody and actually lead to spiritual decline by virtue of rendering life all that much more focused on the physical. When a person is starving, they will seek to placate their hunger. Even spiritual individuals, pacifistic as they may be, and ascetic as they may be, are often unhinged by this biological need and regress to animalism. And if they don't, and times are especially hard, they become easy targets for those of a less pacifistic nature.

The east makes a great show of protecting animals and regarding vegetarianism as morally superior, and pretends to in all aspects be the purest pacifistic pan-societal enclave in existence, yet then we observe, for example, the nation of India building atomic weapons, or the lepers wandering the forests of Asia untreated not because it isn't possible to wipe out leprosy but because no effort at such goals has been seriously made. The east then chastises the west, saying that the ascetic style of Catholicism or something similar is wrong, yet they are unable to see their own errors. Likewise, even if we presume some moral "good" in such pacifism and vegetarianism, it dampens the same cyclical struggles that improve man's understanding of the world. If knowledge is power, then the eastern world has limited its own attainment by virtue of attempting to constantly remove these processes, seeking even on the spiritual level in many cases to escape the reincarnation process that they so believe in. One common criticism of christianity is found in Nietzsche: "The christian resolution to find the world ugly and bad has made the world ugly and bad." We can apply this to the east. Their own resolution to find life miserable has made life miserable, and they seek only to escape the physical world which would be a far more stable, beautiful place to be if they used their massive manpower and organization skills to beautify it. How sad, that they spend so many lifetimes worrying about the hereafter only to reincarnate into the same world made ever less bright and livable by their own denial of the importance of physical life.

OCCULT PHILOSOPHY

It is, however, in their understanding of time that the largest error is made. Geometrically speaking a circle is about the worst representation of time that can be made, specifically because a circle is an imaginary geometric form actually made up of a huge number of equal sides rotating around a central point. If you wish to prove this, just draw a square and an octagon, and then a figure of similar structure (all sides being equal) with 36 sides. The more sides that you add, the more circular it appears. A circle is merely such a figure with the number of sides carrying the imaginary placeholder of infinity that we already discussed. A true circle, then, is simply that same imaginary whole with outer layer "1" with this as the value of its size so that the number of "sides" becomes the placeholder because they become unquantifiable in number.

We cannot represent time in this manner because it is overly simplistic. Perhaps the allusion here made is more to the concept of everything as a totality, fallen from its original homogenized form by some aberrant process; some mention that desire itself was the corrupting influence here, and that desire leads to more desire, and eventually the inability to acquire the desired. Since this is imagined to be the case within these eastern paths (or at least some of them) it is unthinkable that they would attempt to improve the world proactively, since the struggles encountered are not overcome but rather just dealt with. This can be seen as a mightily aberrant force on its own; these individuals are unable to improve themselves through adversity, because adversity, to them, is inconsequential and must be largely ignored. As such they miss many opportunities and can only be harming the same karma they claim to believe in.

In the next passage I will explain how western conceptions are also wrong. The reader should keep in mind that this is not a dichotomy, for both sides compose only a tiny finite portion of all philosophy. There is much that is not entirely contained in either, and there are principles which neither holds which are closer to the truth than either school of thought ever believed in.

OCCULT PHILOSOPHY

WESTERN PHILOSOPHY IS WRONG

Western philosophy represents time as a line or branching line with no cycle present at all. This is at least as wrong as the eastern concept of time, if not worse specifically because it doesn't even resemble a cycle at all. In the mathematical sense, this has caused many a conundrum within science specifically because this poor visual representation forces the greater thinkers to ponder whether the line in question is finite in length (the universe is singular and came into being by some force at a finite spot in time before which there was nothingness.) Or infinite.

Likewise, is it finite in *both* directions? If before the big bang there was "nothing" and thus no time at all, will that same situation come into being at some future finite point, at which even the subatomic particles break down into nothingness and we are once again theoretically left with that same "nothing?" Or, rather, is it finite in reverse, with a discrete point of creation, but now because nothing has become something, time becomes infinite in the future direction with regards to this imaginary line of time?

I explained formerly; such finite mathematics and finite visual representations are great for quantifying the finite, quantifiable reality around us, but when it comes to these larger questions which impact our very notion of existence, they're powerless. The west has additional problems as well with its philosophies. One such problem is more a matter of modern politics- real capitalism which maximizes competition (thus reducing prices and increasing wages) has been replaced by monopolistic corporate entities which experience little outside competition to force them to adapt and improve. This isn't social Darwinism, as the progressives suggest, but is actually an oligarchic mutant. The occult is much the same, with a few large religious orders and spiritual groups attempting in every dishonest manner to suppress smaller or schismatic groups, unable to turn to themselves and ask why, if their philosophy is so grand and noble, there was a schism to begin with.

OCCULT PHILOSOPHY

The west is also obsessed with the concept of making every aspect of the natural world work to their benefit. Were it not for a few forward-thinking individuals every square inch of this world would be carpeted by cement by now and we'd be living already in a wasted dystopia of steel and factory farms. This has been prevented mostly by the efforts of a few organizations and groups which understand that this type of future again makes life all that much harder. To the eastern ascetic it means constant distraction and to the western hedonist it means the inability to actually live the pastoral life, with its fields and ales and fine tobacco, the true hedonistic lifestyle of the epicurean as opposed to the false hedonism of trust funds, sports cars, and mansions which entice the unwise.

Here I can even speak of western conspiracy theories revolving around some occult elite- why on earth would someone "in the know" about such principles seek to live in an urban zone, overseeing monstrous currency exchanges and stock prices and property values, to the exclusion of all personal enjoyment? Rather, those truly in the know regarding the occult despise such things, and indulge in them only far enough to fund their more simplistic enjoyments. If a person finds enjoyment in walking around the forest or whittling a stick or playing with a yo-yo they don't have to worry about the world economy because they can continue such things during the most crippling depression. If, instead, they find enjoyment in swindling people through larger economic systems they may very well find their ultimate enjoyment to be unattainable when things go awry. Here is wisdom; for this is the epicurean ideal.

The east, thus, in wanton asceticism, and the west with its ever present desire to increase wealth, are both misled- neither group fully comprehends totality, and the philosophy of the cycle. The east seeks a nonexistent liberation from cycles, thinking them "bad" when its their own physical action that makes it so, and the west ignores these cycles and focuses on singular and often extravagant endeavors.

OCCULT PHILOSOPHY

The west is further misled by virtue of the misunderstanding of individuality. We are all sovereign beings, and in each incarnated form we inhabit we have an ego separate from others. The east, again, regards this as somehow a bad thing even though its actually natural and desirable, allowing us to experience the world in its many pleasures. The westerner, however, takes this egotism to the extreme and envisions that everything is utterly separated, when really all life stems from one primordial form, and all existence around us is merely differentiated from one singular apocalyptic explosion many billions of years ago. The occult can embrace the big bang whether it is in a theistic form, or merely a spiritual form; for this event could be said to have been the action of a divine hand, or an innate but ultimately ordered process relying on no god but rather some cosmic force we cannot yet comprehend.

The easterner sees all humans as striving to be reconnected with all else in existence, to be homogenized and assimilated into some divine whole. The westerner sees all humans as discrete, separate parts. The westerner is seeing merely a collection of intricate machined devices out of context, when in reality if they stepped back a bit they would be able to see that all of these intricate humans are inextricably connected to one another in various cycles and systems.

I say thus, that the east and west are both half right and half wrong. The easterner is wrong to say we're all meant to be homogenized, and the westerner is wrong when claiming we're all separate forever. The easterner and westerner, if astute, will rather agree that we are separate *but* linked by these cosmic systems, including the capability to reincarnate into one another as egotistical forms. Some believe in the concept of soul-mates (in a literal way, not in the manner of simply two people who like one another very much.) And here the claim is made that two people can be quite literally linked together across many reincarnation cycles. This pairing system is quite obviously possible, although most individuals will romantically claim that whoever they happen to end up with at any time is their soul-mate. The former is reality. The latter is romantic fancy.

OCCULT PHILOSOPHY

NOTHING ENDS AND MORALITY IS SUBJECTIVE

In reality it is *impossible* for the human consciousness, or even the dim consciousness of a lower life form, to stop existing. Reincarnation, in some form, is truth, although there are multiple, valid theories about its manner, some of which I will attempt to explain in some detail here.

It is impossible specifically because when we regard the composition of the dimensions- whether we're discussing my own visual interpretation or that of those who endorse string theory or similar theories- we're left regarding lower dimensions as compositional, finite components of a higher. If this is the case then your entire life is mostly illusory and connected at higher levels with those of other life forms there. We might for example posit a two dimensional life form whose entire existence and reality takes place in a split second overlapping your own physical body- you are not aware of this because this second dimension has no width. Since your own body is a mechanistic, orderly biological system, so too is the entire reality of that second dimensional life form also orderly.

Likewise the ego you possess is spawning an infinite number of realities also. Every thought you have, however bizarre, creates such an existence on other planes, because anything that can be reserved will be reserved. The secularist argues that this can't be true because the mental is an expression of the physical mind. This objection overlooks the fact that since there is still a physical component influencing that mental imagery, it is still able to project into other dimensions, if not in the same exact manner we experience it.

When you die your physical body will, sad as this may be, decay into the dirt and eventually your body will be nothing more than a skeleton surrounded by the withered, dusty remains of your flesh. Or, perhaps, you will be cremated. Or, perhaps, you will die in the forest and be eaten by maggots. The end result is the same; after a million years your body will likely have been atomized more or less and reconstituted into the tissues of other life forms.

OCCULT PHILOSOPHY

Even this macabre recycling process is another such cycle- observe that those living tissues are almost all being taken back up into other life forms. In a four-dimensional way you might say the consciousness you possess is, in a way, also being imparted to these lower beings which are absorbing your flesh. That is not to say it makes you likely to reincarnate as a maggot, but rather that this is yet another system in which life forms connect. I find the eastern belief that humans are able to reincarnate as, say, insects or low life forms a bit strange, and do not pretend to fully believe in this. It seems that a consciousness, once it reaches a truly sentient, sovereign, advanced stage, wouldn't be capable of piloting such a crude vessel any more.

Some speak of the *akashic records* and the persistence of all mental thought-forms on some astral dimension. I think instead that they speak of the fourth dimension and not some other realm of reality. The dimensions, as I view them and as some others do, are actually a scientifically quantifiable arrangement of mathematically overlapping realms, and there is nothing particularly occult about the realms themselves, merely about understanding the arrangement and how it affects existence and spirituality.

This is loosely tied to the concept of the *noosphere* which even contains alchemical philosophy (because transmutation of material components is an eventual product of the process of noogenesis.) I say loosely tied here, mainly because it deals not with a mental realm separate from the physical, but rather the mental aspect *of* the physical. The latter concept, the noosphere as opposed to the akashic records, is closer to being a useful conception of the mental state of mankind and of sovereign life forms, for it allows us to understand the topic without dragging in a realm of existence which so far has yet to be proven exists in a century of philosophical and occult experimentation. Nonetheless, the concept of the akashic records is valid, even if we presume it is impossible for any human regardless of mental training to actually access the fourth dimension in such a way that they can glean anything useful from it.

OCCULT PHILOSOPHY

Anything, however intangible it may seem, will persist and exist both in the higher and lower dimensions. In fact, it is only in the dimension we ourselves physically experience that this isn't the case; our reality is finite because we comprise a finite proportion of the reality. In any lower dimension our finite existence is actually infinite and directly forms reality. In any higher dimension all of our thoughts and physical forms become part of that same intangible whole which would be regarded by a higher life form existing therein- but at the same time we ourselves affect that reality by being a component of it.

That is to say: If I imagine, in my mind's eye, a dragon, I can say, this dragon is a mental image; it has no physical form in the third dimension and here it is not real except in my mind. However, my mind itself comprises a limitless number of existences in the lower dimension, or at least proportional parts of that second dimensional existence. If, then, I am imagining this dragon, it's quite literally present in those lower dimensions- if I imagine a person, and write about them, and create a story, that story is playing out line for line somewhere in the lower cosmos, and is literally, physically real in it. I envision this as being identical to our own reality, and to those life forms it would seem like the third dimension, because *our* dimension is the far grander, larger force that determines its composition. To such a life form, *our* reality encompasses infinite time, and is in a way identical to how we regard the fourth dimension.

As such, by merely imagining that we are immortal, or that reincarnation is real, or that we live forever in some form, it becomes true- and even if we do not, another individual may imagine the same thing and create a similar thought-form which persists on the lower dimensions and comprises a part of the higher, if a very small one. When we look in the mirror, the mental image that we create gazing at our own reflection essentially crafts a clone of ourselves in a similar reality and this as well overlaps the second dimension and perpetuates it. Reality is far more convoluted than most people can possibly imagine.

OCCULT PHILOSOPHY

I say; there was no beginning to our existence. All of these existences have existed forever and always will, because time is thus an illusion. Even the calculations made by the most brilliant physicists comprise only a finite summation of a finite reality, to the direct exclusion of their application to a higher or lower dimension by virtue of their own nature. The only way to work around this concept is to perhaps state that it is possible that existences are spawned by what amounts to the reaction between matter and antimatter on some higher plane. In this we might imagine our entire universe is akin to an atom and that it was spawned when whatever matter and antimatter makes up the fourth dimension collided, releasing virtually inexhaustible amounts of energy here that nonetheless would be a tiny release on the higher.

Some may object and say that thus it is just as possible that there is an afterlife (for example, a heaven or hell that lasts for an infinite period) instead of some ongoing process of reincarnation. This is just as strange and ignores just as much truth about these cosmic cycles as the belief in escaping the process via ascetic practices. If we believe, for a moment, as the christians do, that there is a divine hand behind all creation- a singular male deity usually- then we have to assume such a being would project aspects of itself, unlimited as though this being is- into the creation being made. If this is the case, then why would this being then exempt its own creations from the sort of cycles it has created and kept going for billions of years? This misunderstanding stems from the same source as those held by easterners; namely the world is seen as fallen, degenerate, corrupted, or in some way a bad place to be. Instead of attempting to ameliorate this and create a better world, the easterner thus wants to escape reality altogether, and the abrahamist wants to keep the trappings of physical reality but to cosmically improve them by abstaining from what they imagine to be sins. This is coupled with any of a number of other facets to their spirituality- grace from jesus, faith in jesus, adherence to a specific church dogma, practicing certain occult rituals (for that is what they are) and so forth.

OCCULT PHILOSOPHY

As to the different types of reincarnation, there are several of them to be regarded.

The first is the karmic process- this can be seen, mostly, as a controlled reincarnation. An individual is judged on some possibly arbitrary moral basis as having done right or wrong in life, in different amounts, and their future incarnation is affected by this.

The second is an uncontrolled process- in this form of reincarnation karma is nonexistent or unimportant for the process itself. If this is the case, reincarnation must be purely controlled by overlapping dimensions or may be random altogether.

Then there is a more genuinely occult process- in this a person may or may not (as they wish) attempt to affect their future incarnation through magickal means. This may or may not be affected by karmic forces.

Finally there is the punctuated system, as found in Theosophy or among some eastern groups, in which there is a period between lives in which the person is refreshed (or, as sometimes said, purged) from their physical life. In some circles the spiritual form enjoyed herein lasts many times longer than each physical life, and there may be higher forms than even the astral posited within it.

I object to the use of karma as a measure of the process on the basis that such philosophies are, as any others made by organized religious forces, purely arbitrary- rather, the mental state of the individual, I believe, is the primary arbiter of the following incarnation. If this is the case, then the specific beliefs of the person matter less than their devotion to doing what *they themselves* have determined is right. This entirely eliminates the moral debate which rages in all organized religions over how the reincarnation and karmic processes are affected by lunacy, or mental handicap, or by outside influences seemingly beyond the control of the individual. If the person has no moral guidance and no conception of morality, there is no standard they may be judged by except man's standards in the strictly physical sense.

OCCULT PHILOSOPHY

In fact we must here derive the concept that *all* morality is relative. There are a large number of people in this world that comprehend the notion that man's laws are subjective and based on, at best, protection of life and order and, at worst, protection of dishonesty and the willful desire to shield the corrupt in order to embezzle money. However, most of these same individuals then regard the spiritual and either believe or wish they believed in the notion of unchanging, absolute, objective divine law. One common misconception voiced by abrahamists especially is that in the absence of such an unchanging objective moral system, morality breaks down and man becomes little more than a barbaric ape. This seems to ignore the generally lawful nature of even the most die-hard atheist, who will craft their own similar moral system based on a recognition of logic, instead of a deity governing their actions and desires.

However, spiritual law is indeed subjective. First, we observe that there are thousands of variants of spiritual belief, which often contravene one another utterly; it is impossible, in an objective sense, for any human to do more than assume one of these many paths is true or closest to truth.

Second, we observe that if *as above so below* holds any philosophical and occult weight at all, man's crafted subjective legal frameworks must both reflect and be a reflection of the higher order. Perhaps, then, the pantheists are partially correct and it matters less which deity or group of deities you venerate so long as you do it properly. Long ago I conceived of the notion that these spiritual forces were not governed by the judgment of a tyrannical god but rather that the person's own mentality judges them passively and innately as they die and immediately begin reflecting upon their now past existence in the physical plane- the spiritual component of the ever present notion of one's life flashing before their eyes when they have finally met their demise.

I am certain some will read this and presume that I am suggesting a lack of some divine force. I am agnostic on this topic, but must state emphatically that the lack of a divine judge does not necessarily imply the lack of a divine creative force. The two do not both need to be present or absent in order for the other to be.

OCCULT PHILOSOPHY

It could be that there is also a divine judge that judges alongside our own internalized judgments and renders merely the sentence thereof. We might think of our own mind as a jury which determines our own spiritual verdict and then some outside force as merely some innate (or intelligent) force which renders final judgment only after we have in turn already judged ourselves. I have heard from some tantrics that upon death the individual sees every aspect of their past life, multiplied in sound and fury many times over. It is for this reason that they consider meditation so important, because it is in this days-long state after death, in that mental realm, that they attempt to liberate themselves, or to in some way affect the outcome of the cycle they're about to re-enter over again. In this, there is no specific cosmic judge, but rather it will merely be more or less difficult for them to attain a positive outcome according to how they have lived life- a *de facto* version of karma that nonetheless is slightly different from other variants.

If we envision the cosmos to be orderly then the order we regard here (and the arbitrary nature, thus, of legalism) must also perpetuate on higher levels. If we envision the cosmos to have a more innate, mechanical orderliness not derived from any divine source, this remains true, and those same mechanisms must be at work above as they are below.

Almost all purists will disagree and say that for some reason their path must be true because they have sensed it, or been told by a god or other force, or something of that nature. If, however, the spiritual is subjective, then so too are those experiences. I have often asked christians how they know that their god isn't actually Satan in another form, deliberately feeding them the bible in order to get them to forgo sensual pleasures just to watch them fail over and over at remaining ascetic for his own amusement or how, if their deity is all powerful, they can be sure that same god isn't lying to them to test them and see if they'll ignore some of the more nonsensical materials within christianity. Their only objection, as with all other groups, is either "I know it's true because this book says so" or "I can just sense or feel it to be true." Again, purely subjective measures of reality.

OCCULT PHILOSOPHY

ORDER HAD TO ARISE BY DEFINITION FROM CHAOS

There are some groups which proclaim that the natural, or beneficial, state of existence is actually one of primordial chaos, to the exclusion of most of what we call order. I have heard it explained by one cult to me, that the essential design was originally one of this chaotic "soup" in which there were a host of bubbles of semi-ordered experience. So long as order was contained in this way, beings were able to rest in this sort of chaos and express and experience simply by tapping into these energetically contained units of order, which they used predominantly as a form of wanton enjoyment. This particular group venerated Lilith, and proclaimed that Jehovah was an evil being, which had punctured chaos and ripped this realm apart, creating an orderly expanse which allowed him to control it- literally he had just envisioned a bubble of order in which he alone had control and the other chaotic beings were locked away in foreign dimensions. When he broke this "bubble" open he then gained total power in the physical world, and unleashed horror upon the life forms he generated, by forcing them to compete, differentiating them from one another largely out of malice.

This explanation is as sensible as the opposing judeochristian belief system, but it is also mathematically untenable; a realm of chaos is simply one in which a great number of mathematical functions are fluctuating between various physical laws and lawlessness- if we observe a finite part of the cosmos around us we can mathematically quantify it at least in part and assign numbers and values to most of the bodies and movements therein; a chaos universe, then, is simply one in which these numeric functions are absent and disordered such that prediction of future bodies, their positions and movements, or of the nature of matter itself, becomes impossible. As with an orderly realm, the chaos realm is limitless- even more obviously so, being unconstrained.

However, for chaos to ultimately exist it has to be truly random- and in a random system limitless in size, we have to assume an infinite number of functions are occurring at every infinitely small point in time. Likewise, in a truly random system, we would expect to occasionally see order arise through these random processes. We have here the metaphor of an infinite number of monkeys typing at an infinite number of typewriters eventually producing every book ever written through random chance alone- the majority of this world would be gibberish, but if you had the time to sift through it all you would eventually find a letter-for-letter copy of every document ever written in intelligible form.

Thus, order *had to arise* mathematically speaking. Once it arose, regardless of whether we posit primordial chaos or a primordial ordered but originally disjointed big bang, it had to continue to order itself according to mathematical laws. We might say that if we combine these two beliefs with one another, that the big bang was thus merely the result of chaos being punctured, with or without allusions to Lilith and the veneration of primordial chaos.

Science, however, is very good at quantifying some things, but is unable to answer other queries. Science can quantify various physical and energetic laws which seem stable and constant in the observable universe, but it cannot answer *why* these laws are as they are. I believe that even if we are in the most sterile, atheistic universe imaginable, in which these spiritual forces are merely the result of inter-dimensional interactions, that nonetheless order had some cause other than "it just happens to be this way." To me, this explanation is awfully similar to the abrahamists when asked why your dog died, or something of that nature; a cop-out is used in place of sound reasoning, and with a dazed smile they will just remark that their god works in mysterious ways, or something along those lines, without any substantial explanation, absolving themselves of the responsibility of philosophical thought in the same way the sterile science of today does with things such as the big bang.

OCCULT PHILOSOPHY

Likewise we can explain the very concept of life in this manner. It matters little for this explanation whether the cosmos were divinely crafted or created through this same random process- life had to arise for the very same reason. We might say life can be as rarely created by random processes as possible and it would still have arisen because the expanse of third dimensional space- and thus the amount of it *able* to be occupied, or literally occupied, by ordered matter- is also infinite in scope. Again, we have an infinite number of mathematically derived processes working in tandem, coupled with all of the chemical processes and weather phenomenon necessary for life arising in many locations through chance alone.

This is the wondrous occult truth behind life- for we don't even have to have a deity present in order to posit the existence of magick or of any other occult principle, in so vast a span of space. The abrahamists claim their deity is all-present. What they actually claim here is that their deity is some sort of force that permeates all existence (for it would necessarily overlap all matter in existence) and yet to them the similar principle of the Tao is somehow a negative form of sinful witchery.

This is why we can be sure that there is life elsewhere in the cosmos- not just bacteria or what we would consider unintelligent life, such as primitive photosynthetic algae or some sort of chemotrophic mold, but rather advanced life- life beyond humanity in terms of its technological capabilities as well as sentient life behind ourselves in the same respect. We could wander the universe and would likely find, in the immensity of its scope, a race similar to ours if we were able to search far and wide with any great speed. Science is skeptical but hopeful of this, but the more reasoned minds within science already know that our planet is "about average" in terms of foreign bodies and that there must be billions of planets in the universe roughly the same as ours, which after all is unique only in the fact that we happen to be here to quantify and observe its own natural systems.

OCCULT PHILOSOPHY

The occult has claimed this for centuries. Long before science took the concept of alien life forms seriously the occult had already posited it- thousands of years ago copper age tribes were recording encounters with star people and sky people, which they envisioned quite literally to be humanoid and which came from above- mostly these stories share the astonishing aspect of claiming that these beings were very much like, and interacted with, humans, although they are usually said to be taller and to wield various magickal properties. Whether this is actual magick or technology as seen by the primitive mind has yet to be seen.

I state emphatically; there is life on other planets, there is life at all levels as we comprehend it; the primitive such as bacteria or life forms without volition and consciousness. There is sentient but less intelligent life, along the lines of how we would view most animal life forms. There is sovereign life similar to ourselves in capacity and understanding, and finally there is advanced life beyond our capabilities which may very well know of our existence and avoid us specifically because we're too lowbrow for them to consider important, or perhaps they see us as warmongering, or perhaps (and this would be the most amusing of all) they worry that their presence would destroy our world specifically because we have so many bizarre egotistical beliefs that would be shattered if we knew advanced life persisted elsewhere. We could also frightfully imagine that advanced life tends to drive itself to extinction over time through war or some other process- this has been alluded to by science as well, which claims that if we find the ruins of any alien civilization but no live aliens to go with them we must presume a high mathematical likelihood that life forms tend to destroy themselves in time- which bodes poorly for mankind, of course.

It is always interesting to surmise that there is an advanced alien being out in the cosmos- perhaps not too distant from our own location- staring at our world on some sort of viewing device, wondering what our primitive minds think about. To the occult this isn't so strange and impossible after all.

OCCULT PHILOSOPHY

To those occultists who would scoff (or who are unconcerned with such musings) I would ask why they have ignored mathematics in their study- observe simply the bell curve and presume that Earth, as we now essentially know is the case, is somewhere near the middle of the bell curve when it comes to habitability and composition. We must then presume that whatever primordial conditions here specifically led to life are present elsewhere. In the scope of billions of years which we speak of it's possible that somewhere life arose a few million years before it did here and has experienced fewer cataclysms but more competition and is now beyond our capability of even comprehending, able to traverse galaxies at will with ease. Until the last decade we thought our planet was special because we could not readily observe bodies similar to ours in size and mainly saw only gas giants. We now know this was due to our own technological capabilities, not to our planet actually being very unique other than it's being dotted with life forms from top to bottom.

Even if this cosmic mechanism- the universe- is truly alone and multiverse theory is wrong, we're still regarding billions of planets like ours, and yet there are occultists, who should know better and have at least a decent grasp of mathematics and the sciences of geology, chemistry, and so forth, who deny that life can exist elsewhere. Why this is the case I cannot be sure, nor can anyone, for the reasons given range from the spiritual to the physical, to simply regard for any foreign intelligent life as little green man conspiracy theories to thus be denied only because of their bad reputation. I do not speak of little green men, I speak of an entire pantheon of advanced beings scattered around the universe and even more numerous life forms of a lower state. I am even willing to advance the theory that many of these life forms would either resemble life on our own planet or would even be capable, technically, of living here, specifically because the number of means of movement and energy gathering are limited- beings get their energy from the sun, or from predation, or from breaking down dead organic matter which still contains molecules able to be broken down at a positive net energy level, or chemotrophs using heat and certain chemical systems, and finally radiotrophs. The presence of extremophile life forms on our planet deep in the Earth and in volcanic and arctic regions expands the habitability of the cosmos.

OCCULT PHILOSOPHY

I will thus claim that there are photosynthetic (or other sun-gathering) life forms on other planets. I claim that cell structure is probably similar in some ways, and that the types of organic arrangements we see in life here exist specifically because they are advantageous and competitive. If competition is existing on other bodies (as it must because of natural selection) then alien beings may resemble those we see here- a tree is shaped the way it is specifically because it has experienced millions of years of competition and is designed in such a way through this selection that it gathers as much energy as possible, as much water too, and every part and function therein is maximized for its specific region in a given time period, changing slowly in accordance with outside stimuli through this selection.

The same selections being at work on any other planet (to the exclusion of a planet terraformed entirely through artificial means by especially advanced beings, which must also have happened elsewhere at some time I am sure) any similar beings are likely to also have arranged themselves similarly because the nature of competition is similar. Science fiction envisions a host of foreign alien beings which are phantasmagorical and grotesque and riddled with vestigial appendages and seemingly contradictory organic facets just to make them seem fearsome or especially intimidating- this is pure nonsense.

What then does this have to do with the occult? There are two points to be made. First, we are not alone, and our egotism is misplaced when it is given a divine importance. Second, and especially if the span of the third dimension is limitless, almost anything is technically possible and almost any form of life you can imagine already exists. If, thus, things are above as they are below, then we may believe that this situation is similar to those on other dimensions and that there are higher forms of life above even the most advanced we could find in our cosmos, and that spiritual forces are very much real indeed, because there is no reason to exclude them from existence when we have at best a mediocre understanding of our realm, let alone others.

OCCULT PHILOSOPHY

YOU COULD MELT ANY OBJECT INTO A SUBATOMIC SOUP AND COBBLE IT INTO ANY OTHER OBJECT INCLUDING AN ATOM FOR ATOM CLONE OF YOURSELF: WHAT DOES THIS SAY ABOUT THE SOUL AND EGO AND DEATH?

In theory even matter itself is fairly interchangeable. Again, this ever present correspondence between the spiritual and physical comes to mind; there is no difference, really, between your own body and that of a spider, or between the spider and a brick of clay, other than the form and number and arrangement of atoms they are composed of. If, however, you developed the energetic means to break down those same atoms into their component subatomic particles- protons, neutrons, and electrons- and reassembled them into different atoms and then into molecules all the way into a solid object, it would become possible to transmute matter itself in the most purely alchemical manner (as has been done by colliding particles at great speed in a particle accelerator, creating gold from nickel or lead) thus creating, say, a bar of gold where there was once a log.

The fact that this has not actually been done outside of a few particles smashed together in an accelerator does not mean it is impossible- nay it is known to be possible because it has thus been done. We may lack the capability to do so easily or at profit, but it is physically able to be done. The transmutation process of the alchemists *is real* and yet the average occultist, uninterested in anything more than their altar and books, remains unawares that this has been performed by science!

See now; science has always followed the occult. The alchemist of the Renaissance was the direct, exact precursor of the chemist of the 19th century and of the physicist of today. The shaman of antiquity is now the pharmacist and biochemist. The ancient berserker has been mechanized and turned into a host of killing gear mass produced for the sole purpose of waging war. There is no uniqueness, as far as we can see, to the particles which compose all matter- therefore, what does this say about the ego?

OCCULT PHILOSOPHY

It means that your ego is very likely illusory- this does not, however, mean that upon physical death your ego disappears. It actually indicates the opposite.

Much like the nickel particle has stopped existing when shot through the accelerator into other atoms and been transmuted into gold, so too does your ego stop existing as it is, only to become something else. Even more happily this process is reversible, and can be performed in different ways an infinite number of times- the limitless expanse of space entails limitless possible energy and matter, and this allows for limitless existence. Your soul, too, as we conceive of it (although ego or consciousness is ultimately a more fitting, less abrahamic term for this) is also limitless.

You could dissolve a human being into subatomic soup and then build them back up again atom for atom- would this then be the same human being or would it be a different one? This question is a modernized, more complicated version of the classic logical scenario in which a ship is slowly repaired over time until every original part has at some time been replaced. It looks exactly like the original ship, with every plank and oar and sail in the same place, made of the same type of material- yet the original pieces used are no longer present. Is it, thus, the same ship, or is it a different ship?

In the sense of the dissolved human we're positing that the subatomic soup was made up of the same particles they originally held. This would perhaps be more akin to taking the ship apart and rebuilding it like a puzzle. Surely, we would say, it is the same puzzle- so too is it the same human. Here is the conundrum- will they possess their former memories and be really, truly, the same ego, or will they be somehow different on a spiritual or mental level, and what then of the "soul?"

OCCULT PHILOSOPHY

I claim here: it is the exact same being you had before. Their ego is held within the confines of a specific body and you have just perfectly replicated it. The period they spent dissolved will, to them, seem only similar to the process of passing out or sleeping without dreaming- an infinitely short span of time, to them, because they were not aware to witness its duration. Additionally, this three dimensional body being inhabited as it were by this specific ego persisted on the fourth dimension, where we might expect the actual "soul" exists, as opposed to simply mental functions of the ego.

Now there is a further mental problem to think of. What if we create an exact replica of the person from inanimate matter, such that we have two atom-for-atom beings which are exactly, perfectly alike? Will they share the same memories, traits, and volition? Will they then proceed to know the others' actions regardless of distance, reacting to stimuli in exactly the same manner?

It is impossible to know, without actually doing so; but I argue "no" specifically because they are not composed of the same matter as the first person, and it seems impossible that they would share the same "soul." We could though posit this to be possible- if the soul is somehow an energetic or upper-dimensional form which simply requires a specific style of mental body to inhabit as a sort of mechanical third dimensional vessel. If this is the case the soul could control two bodies at once. However, in the dimensional arrangement scheme I have envisioned only the body made from the same particles it was to begin with is intricately connected together on the higher dimension, while the one composed of formerly inanimate matter is connected to a pile of logs, or rocks, or ingots of iron, or some other collection it was crafted from to begin with. We have thus created not a sovereign being, but a fully autonomous organic *golem* of sorts- and yes, here too this strange tale of the golem can be regarded as true. I predict that in the future melting objects and reforming them in a powerful energetic field will not only be possible, it will be considered easy to do in laboratory conditions, if not in one's own home, assuming man is not wiped out by war, disease, or celestial impact from some foreign body like an asteroid.

OCCULT PHILOSOPHY

OCCULT PHILOSOPHY

PSYCHOTROPICS HAVE DONE MORE FOR THE WORLD THAN ANYTHING ELSE

Now we come to a further topic neglected in some schools of the occult. Actually, when we consider some groups, the importance of psychotropics isn't ignored so much as abhorred, although it's clear some groups involve themselves with this prohibition style stance specifically to avoid legal cases and to absolve themselves of responsibility for the experimentation of their adherents.

Psychotropics have played a penultimate role in the development of spirituality and religion; we get the image of the tree of Eden treated as a psychedelic mushroom in some medieval and renaissance era paintings and sketches, and we get references to the *soma* which has been claimed as psilocybin. Psychotropics have experienced several ages- another oscillation which includes both declining and expanding usage and importance, according to the culture and its ethos on such things at the time. In the modern era, as of this writing, we are leaving an era of relative apprehension and prohibition and entering one in which tolerance of such usage is expanding quickly- perhaps more quickly than at any time since far antiquity.

In the distant past man appears to have used psychotropics with great frequency- we find little prohibition of their use amongst most still-primitive tribes in the world, and ceremonial use of the same is quite common, especially amongst the Yanomami and Masai people- the former in the Amazon basin, the latter in Africa.

The proper term for the use of such substances in a spiritual rather than recreational context is *entheogen.* In modern times some westerners and easterners alike still believe (wrongly) that the consumption of any mind altering substance not prescribed by a doctor is somehow being used solely for illicit purposes, even though most such species have a medical or divine purpose.

OCCULT PHILOSOPHY

There is far more wisdom to be gleaned from psychotropics than any prohibition-supporting group can understand; the natives who inhabited North America at the time the colonists came must have been astonished that they drank alcohol yet condemned the ingestion of various spiritually significant herbs. I have studied the archaeology of the Caribbean (which is its own small sub-school within archaeology) and the number of psychotropics ingested by some of the tribes there was extreme; in fact, much like the Masai warriors, it's rather strange that we hear few if any cases of overdose considering the quantities involved are so high.

Almost always these substances played a direct spiritual role; only in the modern age does there seem to be a problem with addiction to such things with the exception of alcohol which was always understood as something one could become habituated to. There are inscriptions at Pompeii that attest to the importance of alcohol within the buried culture there- inscriptions revolving around the price of drinks and how drunk certain citizens became before crudely inscribing the same on the outside walls of their home or on the inside of a bar.

One ever-present allusion in the modern period has been that of "machine elves" as it has been termed by McKenna, who along with Timothy Leary and a few others were among the most advanced minds of their age. Political views aside the spiritual component of entheogens which they rediscovered had been mostly absent from the western world until the 1960s and into the 1970s, although some substances had entered the public consciousness before then- how odd, that opiates became popular in the west before psilocybin came into wide use. This may have even spiritually corrupted the cultures themselves because people became addicted to harder substances without the benefit of those which are more spiritually aware and spiritually expanding.

I have partaken, myself, in numerous substances of this sort- morning glory seeds, salvia, psilocybin, mescaline, blue lotus, amanita mushrooms, syrian rue, the famed *ayahuasca* and so forth- each one has a different psychedelic spirit of sorts, and I must describe these spirits here to the best of my ability.

OCCULT PHILOSOPHY

In this I have to acknowledge a truth- different people respond differently to different substances. The classic psychoaut explanation for this is merely that people have different vibrations or states of mind and that they affect people differently as a result of this alone; I believe it goes further than just this sort of secular observation and that the substances are sacraments of a sort which represent different aspects of the spiritual cosmos themselves. As such, people may find that one substance admits them into full harmony with the teaching it is able to impart, while another may get only a partial glance thereof, and a third person might have a particularly poor experience with a specific substance and glean little or nothing in the way of enlightened wisdom from it.

I had always been told by others who indulged in psychedelics that LSD was more difficult than psilocybin, for example; they claimed that LSD was harsher, stronger, and that the "come down" (decline of the experience after 4 to 6 hours) was particularly difficult, while with psilocybin the "come up" was a bit more difficult but ultimately the substance was easier to make use of. I found the exact opposite to be true in my own experience; psilocybin was almost mind warping especially with respect to its capability to make time seem to slow down, and LSD was conversely extraordinarily relaxing, bringing on a long-lived meditative state, for me, which lasted more or less the entire duration of the trip, and which was entirely enjoyable. On psilocybin, though, I became overwhelmed by the sensory experience and attempted to darken the room and ride it out through meditation only to temporarily become worried that I had injured myself because I kept seeing blood on my hand that to me looked entirely real.

The first substance I used for spiritual purposes was morning glory- I do not understand why this has been so overlooked since it was the purest spiritual experience of all. It contains ergine and LSA- substances related to LSD but less potent than it. This overlooked plant is commonly grown in gardens, although in my northern climate it rarely grows long enough to produce usable seeds without getting frosted- early frost kills the seeds and they essentially ferment, releasing alcoholic foam as they rot.

OCCULT PHILOSOPHY

The nature of morning glory is unique from a spiritual perspective- it's not the same as the similar LSD molecule, and the differences are more than subtle here; morning glory invites the meditative, relaxed, slightly euphoric state of LSD but lacks the visual impact. LSD causes color changes, size warping, and other similar effects, but the LSA and ergine present in morning glory does not.

Morning glory worked best, in my own experience, as a meditation aid, although some people seem to experience mild confusion while under its effects. The minutiae of the world is far more interesting while under its spell, and the general power that it gives isn't one of a mind bending portal into other dimensions so much as an introspective one. Here I will theorize; there are psychedelics that are *internalizing* and those which tend to be *externalizing*. This is by no means an indication that any psychedelic can't be used for either purpose and again some individuals respond differently to different psychedelics, but some *tend* to create an internal experience, one which is introspective, meditative, or relaxing, and others thrust you into other realms of imagination.

My first psychedelic experience with the seeds was taken at night on a dose of about 250 seeds- a fairly small dose, but one which is effective, and some have said that as little as 100 seeds cause at least mild effects. There's a concept spoken of in some folklore of "morning glory heaven" which is this same altered state of mind, wherein people (typically small children) encourage one another to ingest them and trip out- I obviously don't condone children using psychedelics, but I haven't heard that small doses of morning glory are any more harmful than a very small amount of marijuana or alcohol, and most psychedelics (morning glory chief here) have little to no addiction potential.

In my first psychedelic experience I attained an altered state of mind which could almost be likened to tribal- it was far more spiritualism than psychedelia so-called, and I found myself crouching over a lamp half naked while sketching things I thought of in my minds' eye- I am not skilled in art, but on morning glory it was a simple matter to do so.

OCCULT PHILOSOPHY

Although morning glory contains LSA (Lysergic Acid Amide) it seems that it's actually the ergine which gives the more psychedelic effects and that LSA is predominantly a relaxant and meditative substance- at higher doses morning glory and other similar species (hawaiian baby woodrose and *rivea corymbosa* in particular) become more and more visual, and at some point there is a cutoff after which they don't seem able to become more so, possibly because the active ingredients at some point maximize absorption and it is impossible to take more into the brain, leading to some of the chemicals being wasted in the body.

I have heard, too, of people taking the fresh flowers and steeping them in distilled water to ferment, eventually creating a sort of wine with mild alcoholic and psychedelic properties but I'm not sure how much of this is real and how much is urban legend, and I can't imagine the flavor is particularly palatable. Likewise, the seeds can be crushed and extracted into simple distilled water, but this endeavor is more difficult than simply grinding the seeds to powder and ingesting them in something like applesauce.

The internalized morning glory experience tends to be blissful. In my time experimenting with this and other substances I connected with dozens of other psychonauts (some in the real world, some on the internet only) and several had tried it, saying that for them it was a difficult and mostly unpleasant time. The only unpleasant part within my own ingestion of the seeds were the frequent leg cramps that go along with the vasoconstriction which morning glory can sometimes cause. Anyone wishing to talk to machine elves or see things flash different colors will not attain their desire using morning glory or any similar ergine containing substances- thankfully though the seeds themselves are legal to own and can be bought anywhere, although almost every company sprays them with fungicides as a seed preservative and most psychonauts grow their own or, if that isn't possible, they will obtain them in bulk from a reliable organic source.

OCCULT PHILOSOPHY

Marijuana is another substance of note- it was used in ancient times by the Scythians although I have found it to be mostly lacking in spiritual importance and honestly don't understand why people use it with such great frequency. This is not to say I oppose its use strictly speaking- and as a medicine it is quite powerful for relieving pain- but ingesting it regularly can cause various behavioral issues.

Higher doses on potent strains are more likely to cause visual effects when using cannabinoids, although these pale in comparison to even weaker psychedelic substances like ergine. Lower doses cause no such effect at all and lead to the stereotypical "laughing at your fingers and eating junk food" or else "nodding off while watching old movies" effects instead. In this way I'm not sure we can class marijuana as anything beyond a medically important substance with a low enough potency and toxicity so that it should never have been made illegal- this dream is coming true, and more parts of the world have finally stopped throwing people in prison for the terrible crime of using a plant that has been used by man for several thousand years or more.

Marijuana though is not particularly psychedelic. In the post-prohibition age the media has made a great big deal about reporting on any death in Colorado or Washington (where it has been legalized) in which the person who crashed their car or did something else of a dumb nature, was also on marijuana at the time. The fact that a hundred other people crashed their cars that day alone and were sober made me chuckle when the reports came out, and I was left wondering why so many supposedly intelligent individuals were so worried about a "possible" case of marijuana causing an accident when thousands of times more such situations are created by perfectly legal alcohol, which is far more addictive, far more toxic, and is almost a part of every culture around the world. Moralist-era temperance dogma seems a fairly likely source for this strange hypocrisy, but these same folks were also the ones that told men to shave their long hair in the 1920s for no other reason than it was supposedly "manly."

OCCULT PHILOSOPHY

Psilocybin is a more interesting substance- in my own use it allowed me to view a sort of matrix around myself from which the world was composed. I began to notice how under its influence objects ran together and appeared to be composed of intricate, fluctuating fields of energy which connected to and repulsed one another selectively. This took the form of an enormous dome around my own body- an aura of sorts- entirely made of crystal and some sort of energetic grid bent around like a sphere which to me looked awfully like a spiders' web. This visual recognition followed in the wake of the more traditional melting and color shifting of objects in which floors and ceilings turn into a sort of colorful goo.

It was at that moment that the liquefied floor gave way to the cathedral of crystal around me that I "broke through" to use the most commonly understood psychedelic term- upon taking a high enough dose of certain substances it is possible to almost entirely liberate oneself from the physical realm and push your mind into a totally separate state in which the physical reality around you is no longer noticed or just barely. Anyone who has studied Tolkein's elf lore has imagined seeing something similar I believe to what I saw under the influence of psilocybin for a fairly brief period of time before the power of the experience was too great for me, even though at this point I had already used other substances with some frequency. I had seen Charles Manson's face floating across my leg in a sort of three dimensional pattern as well, and at that point I decided it was time to try to internalize the experience again but this failed and I spent several hours in a state where I honestly can't remember what I saw other than the numbers on my clock warping and changing colors.

This liberated state is fundamentally similar to that attained by years of meditation- however the latter is to be preferred generally because it has other benefits that even medically potent psychedelics may not have. It is, however, always interesting when physical objects begin to bend, shake, vibrate, and melt, and a higher dose allows one to quite literally hear the song of the spheres once they envision the sphere they themselves have around them.

OCCULT PHILOSOPHY

Salvia Divinorum is in a league of its own as to its potency. When it first began to enter the public consciousness that there was a legal substance which caused utterly absorbing full hallucinations, naturally the media did the same thing that it had formerly done with MDMA or would do later with e-cigarettes. That is, the media attempted to crucify it.

I can remember when the local paper claimed someone had taken the substance and promptly built an altar in their living room composed of a charcoal grill (which they lit) and various flammable substances, causing them to die of smoke inhalation and nearly burn down their home. Not once was a proper name given, not once was the story sourced to a legitimate agency, not one was even the specific town mentioned; it was just a generic, propagandized story almost certainly crafted by a rogue journalist and then passed off as real to some other agency, which disseminated it without checking to make sure it was real.

Years later we finally got the real story- the teen in question had indeed killed himself through using a grill to asphyxiate himself, but was not high at the time, with the salvia no more an obvious prompt to the suicide than any other random object nearby, other than that it happened to be a "scary" substance that every soccer mom was worried about. He wasn't even in a living room and hadn't "built an altar" either- he had rigged up a tent in the garage and offed himself. The actual salvia experience tends to prevent the user from actually doing anything beyond crawling or making noises or laughing uncontrollably- and therefore it seems impossible that someone on such a substance would have been able to rig up a tent and light the grill to kill themselves, especially since the experience lasts at most 15 minutes, and often a shorter period- not long enough to light up and erect a tent when the tent has probably at that point warped into an octopus.

OCCULT PHILOSOPHY

There is a man called Rob Gonzalves who has been painting fine art for some time- if an uninitiated individual wants to see the sorts of things one sees on salvia, his art depicts it perfectly, although I'm not sure that he has used the substance or any other. As far as visual power goes, salvia is, bar none, more powerful than any other. Stronger than LSD, stronger than even a high dose of psilocybin, and stronger even than mescaline.

In fact the experience is at least somewhat similar to that of the equally famed DMT which I never tried in its pure form (regrettably, as I had attempted to obtain it several times.) I did though brew ayahuasca on one occasion, getting a weak effect from my efforts which is barely worth mentioning other than it did cause a massive purge- which is why it is termed *la purga* since the strong vomiting is unavoidable. Salvia, then, was something I used fairly frequently for some time, alongside morning glory, thus getting the internal and external experience for some months.

On salvia, it makes perfect sense that your bed should suddenly turn into a gigantic window that you're crouching on looking at an entire planet rotating quickly below you. It also makes sense to you at the time that your computer's keys should suddenly turn into a cobblestone road that you are then sucked into by sideways gravity, being told that you need to go and slay the turtle king- in fact it made sense to me, because those are just a few of the things that happened when I used it. Beyond the purely amusing aspect of such things there is a deeper spiritual capability- salvia allows one to see the fractal design behind the entire dimension, not just to commune with life forms on some other plane. Much like DMT often leads to the user meeting reptilian aliens or machine elves, salvia often causes physical objects to take up a sentient form, even interacting with the one who has imbibed the salvinorin itself- for my part I didn't just thus meet the turtle king, but also a succubus (as those who use the term black magick would term it) and a particularly mischievous Shiva, who turned himself into a sort of court jester and proceeded to juggle balls of fire while a Hindi chant melted away into smoke leaving only an extremely interesting tribal drum beat.

OCCULT PHILOSOPHY

Mostly, mainstream culture looks at such things and merely says "those are not real, they are hallucinations." I ask then, is this experience much different from those who have seen the virgin Mary or any other divine creature? Perhaps mainstream, culture has it wrong and these substances and their use lead directly, in some cases, to seeing such fantastic things. This is almost surely the case in medieval times when people tended to eat baked goods which from time to time were tainted with ergot- the mold which is used to make LSD and which has its own psychedelic (and harmful) properties.

Likewise, in antiquity people often either deliberately ingested such intoxicants or else spun stories which seem to indicate their use. The same blue lotus I ingested is almost unarguably the basis for Homer's tale of the island of lotus eaters- even the effects are similar, from the laziness to the forgetfulness, for blue lotus is a pure hypnotic intoxicant and traditional recipes call for it to be steeped in wine, which would have surely been the method used in that past time period. Much like archaeology has delved into antiquated epics and plays and found truth in them (such as with Troy which had been considered mythical prior to its rediscovery by Schliemann) so too should psychonaut culture attempt to delve into the same to find these connections to the spiritual use of various mind altering substances. Of note here is that most psychotropics are probably still not directly known by science, for every few years a new substance seems to be "discovered" despite having been used for centuries or thousands of years by some ancient culture. There are thousands of fungal and photosynthetic life forms waiting in jungles and deserts and mountains in the world that have not even been discovered by science, and some will obviously have such properties.

Here I must state; I oppose "stoner" culture and things of that nature specifically because it tries to relegate spiritually important substances and life forms to the realm of mere entertainment. I have to presume that the western governments themselves had a hand in creating such subcultures specifically to combat the growing concern they had that pot smoking hippies would discover ancient lore and become a gigantic pacifistic religion opposed to authoritarianism.

OCCULT PHILOSOPHY

Then too we have mescaline- and this is an interesting substance because the active chemical is not just found in peyote but also in perfectly legal cacti such as the san pedro, which is used in landscaping in the south and southwest with great frequency because of its ease of growth- anyone can grab one and stick it in the ground and it will tend to grow on its own with little help until it's ten feet tall. The fact that a ten foot segment of san pedro is enough to create about 20 doses of purified mescaline seems to have avoided notice by most of the people growing them.

I never had any desire to "purify" what I saw as spiritually significant substances though, and ended up simply obtaining dried cactus stars, which are sold for decorative purposes with the real purpose being thinly veiled. After grinding them into a fine powder I added them to lemon juice and allowed them to become a sort of slimy green goo which was horrible in flavor- exceptionally bitter and yet also exceptionally sour- and which nearly caused me to vomit. Mescaline has a nature different from similarly powerful psychedelics- and it might be one of the most strictly positive experiences I had.

The main effect was a tingling up and down the spine- very pronounced in its strength, which lasted for several hours. It felt as though every spinal segment was being energized and massaged- the visual impact was pronounced but secondary. I was inside at the time and the ceiling wafted to and fro like thin clouds in a desert sky. I do not know whether this was a more externalized hallucination or whether it was internal and I was imprinting my imagination on my surroundings- because in the mid winter indoor environment I very much wished I had been outside under the clouds instead of cramped up in a dorm where it was warm.

Here I must return briefly to the subject of state drug prohibition and "drug education" (so called) to relate a particularly funny story.

OCCULT PHILOSOPHY

This story is one of a speaker who came in to talk to us dumb, uneducated students in high school about his high knowledge involving drugs. This man, whoever he was, had supposedly been into using such substances as the Devil's weed (marijuana) and Satan's cactus (peyote) among other seemingly demonic photosynthetic life forms. (Satan is almost always invoked when prohibition-happy authoritarians propagandize to a fresh batch of captive audience students in one of your local schools- just say no kids!)

First he indicated that he had taken "peyote root" which is a nonexistent drug because the peyote button is the part of the plant actually used. Then when I asked him if he supported medical marijuana usage he said no, because people can always use morphine... Morphine, which is derived from the same opiate poppy as heroin and is both highly addictive and massively toxic at high doses.

That this was probably a random man who got paid fifty dollars to come in and lie to people presumably too young to realize it was clear at the time and remains clear now. I was sent to the office once for chuckling about propaganda when the TA handed out a little story about some generic teen who smoked marijuana and eventually became a heroin addict because of it, ending up nearly dying after having been such a promising, intelligent young upstanding man. That one toke on his first joint quickly ruined his entire life and he ended up HIV positive, addicted to heroin, and a complete mess whose friends invariably abandoned him after realizing his state. This is pure propaganda and not based on reality, and I will say here something to keep in mind; I live in an extremely liberal state where marijuana has now been decriminalized and the curriculum is 100% secular- and yet this was the swill we listened to, often from people who themselves had never seen a drug in real life or who were hypocrites who themselves probably used marijuana. I can think of a few teachers and professors who, it is common knowledge, had the occasional voluntary run-in with the Devil's weed.

OCCULT PHILOSOPHY

Prohibition is nothing less than an attempt by moralist abrahamists to control people's spiritual beliefs by jailing those who break free from convention and obtain substances which might actually improve their way of life or their way of thinking- coupled of course with the need to criminalize as many things as possible to keep their several millions of slaves in work camp labor behind the steel bars of our prisons. This strange situation has the cartels and the police in widespread agreement; legalizing any of these substances reduces the income of both groups.

Not all hope is lost though- a lot of these plants and fungi are legal on their own specifically because they're found in nature- such as amanita mushrooms (specifically the fly agaric.) This substance was exceedingly strange, because the dose used is the only differentiation between a psychedelic and a delirium-tainted trip. At high doses, it becomes an outright deliriant and causes full-immersion hallucinations more potent than anything other than salvia or possibly psilocybin, and far less pleasurable than either. At lower doses it is merely a psychedelic, but a unique one with its own strange nature.

I took fly agaric caps half a dozen times. Two of these times it had no noticeable effect (including one usage of a dose which should have caused delirium.) Once, I attained a delirious state followed by a purge. Three of these times I attained instead the much lauded psychedelic state, in which the body feels warm and weightless and objects glow and shine like they're laden with gold leaf- it's a spectacularly positive experience unless the dose is too high and delirium sets in, because once the purge occurs the experience swiftly wanes. These caps, dried properly, used to be relatively inexpensive and readily available as imports from Latvia and Russia or from Washington State but sellers have lately disappeared, probably because the revenue is limited at best from their sale, since to my knowledge drug law hasn't changed regarding this fungus, which grows wild across most of the Pacific Northwest, New England, up into Canada on both sides, and in various parts of Europe and Asia.

OCCULT PHILOSOPHY

These substances and others have all been used in ritualism around the world at some time or another- salvia didn't even enter into the US in any large quantities until someone realized the Mazatecs down in the Oaxaca area used it regularly. In the 1960s word of mouth and hippie and anarchist literature was the primary means by which drug knowledge moved around (leading to the entire "bananadine" hoax being taken seriously for so long) but in the modern day and age we have the internet, where knowledge that once would have taken months or years to disseminate can be spread worldwide in a matter of days or hours, if it finds the right avenue to do so. This has been the case with certain coleus species as well, amongst other substances.

The wave of consciousness that swept the west during the period of roughly the end of the 1950s to the middle of the 1970s was one brought on largely by psychedelics. Were it not for these substances, a great deal of music and art and political change that was present in this era would not have existed- we need look no further than Woodstock, acid-drenched and filled with hazy clouds of marijuana and baskets full of mushrooms and cactus to see the result of this mass awakening; for it would not have been an iconic concert at all if extremely high hippies weren't wandering aimlessly around between shows skinny dipping and talking about the trees talking to them.

The very concept within the public that finally crushed the war effort was partly the result of people who were using psychotropics- it was a re-balancing effect, in a culture that had previously been largely in favor of war and segregation. The new age of spirituality, combined with the resurgence of paganism and occultism among the larger mainstream population, then, was like a cart full of fireworks, and psychotropics could be seen as the single match that set them all off around the same time. Around this time, we get the Temple of Set, the Church of Satan, and various splinter orders. We get the Werewolf Order, a new wave of Thule and Atlantean materials, Wicca grows rapidly, Norse mythology continues to grow in importance from this period through the 1980s and into the modern era with various sagas and so forth.

OCCULT PHILOSOPHY

As of the very time of this writing the Icelandic people have begun planning a new pagan temple- the first truly modern pagan center of worship to be constructed in centuries- it is being crafted by the Asatru, and will honor Odin and Frigg. The fact that paganism has grown prevalent enough for a nation with a population as small as that of Iceland, to construct such a temple, is monumentally important.

As the world secularizes, psychotropics are on the forefront of replacing aging, outdated abrahamic doctrine with more forward-thinking modern dogma- oddly enough most of these forces are similar to pagan forms that existed centuries or thousands of years ago- I say *oddly* only because the average abrahamist would wonder why this is happening. Why, after so many centuries of christian and islamic dominance, are the old religions they tried to destroy suddenly eclipsing their own growth? The answer is simple- the cosmic oscillation favored religion spread by sword during the era when struggle was maximized on a cultural and social level- the purification through struggle forced these religious forces to compete through warfare.

In the modern age, though, this has become largely absent- the purification has already completed, as to physical struggle, and now the mental struggle begins. A secularized pagan religion which regards nature and tribal practice will out-compete a religion that only exists because people killed one another to spread it beyond current borders. In this way, paganism embraces modern cultural doctrine and is able to out-compete religions that no longer have the blessing of most states to physically oppress those who exempt themselves from jewry, christianity, and islam.

That is, we might think of this as an oscillation lasting centuries, between religions which are more mentally adept, and religions that are more physically forceful. The physically forceful religions oppress the intelligent, natural ones, forcing them to purify themselves through struggle. At the same time, the forceful religions are in turn purified during gentler, more intelligent ages, by being forced to modernize to stay somewhat relevant.

OCCULT PHILOSOPHY

Psychotropic usage opens gates to foreign realms- the atheists understand this concept as well as any mystically-minded individual although they label it mental and not spiritual force that is being absorbed through the use of said substances. Ultimately, psychotropics are essentially *whatever the user regards them to be.* The occultist will use these substances to commune with what they regard as spirits or deities or other forces of a cosmic, intelligent nature. The secularist may use them for mental insight- more than one brilliant innovator or writer has done this. Those opposed to psychotropics all too often present them in spiritual terms anyways; the devil's weed, the devil's apple, or some other evil, demonic plant or fungus that bewitches the mind and leads those ingesting it to an early grave to be enslaved forever by Satan.

But Satan has little to do with these things- the ingestion of psychotropics have more often been seen as positive than negative events by most of the religious groups we've seen through human history, and even those who shun them publicly often use them privately, specifically because it is an unspoken secret amongst them that such substances inspire and turn the mind inwards or outwards, allowing people to think in ways they otherwise could not.

The occult is concerned with medicine as well, and healing- for this psychotropics are often better than anything else. Psychedelics can lift the mood temporarily or (some claim) permanently, and they can heal trauma and prevent or ameliorate stress more easily than the pharmaceuticals prescribed to patients in our hospitals. We here have to differentiate between conditions which primarily affect the lifespan or physical health- almost invariably treated more easily by non-herbal, western methods, especially with regards to a virus, and conditions which are mainly mental or chronic which are almost always more easily cured or treated through the use of herbalism and occultism. Herbalism does poorly against influenza but is very good at alleviating pain associated with it. Western medicine does well at conquering a virus but usually prescribes dangerous processed opiate synthetics for all variants of pain- addictive, liver-harming substances easily replaced by a dozen different psychotropic substances.

OCCULT PHILOSOPHY

Here we have to take one final facet of psychotropics (or more appropriately, mind altering substances in general) into mind- specifically as they relate to US culture, for prohibitions on alcohol, which is mostly used for recreation despite having some spiritual potential, ended long, long before any easing of psychedelic prohibition even became part of modern discourse. Psychedelics may have come into wider use circa the mid to late 1960s but remained prohibited, while alcohol had only fairly briefly been outlawed before the public made it impossible to continue such a practice.

In fact we might consider that our particular culture has relegated alcohol specifically to culture and divorced it of spirituality; more intervention and regulation of alcohol has been developed in the last few decades even as psychotropics have become more generally tolerated- marijuana is just the first of many such substances which will, I predict, become medically legal at first, and later decriminalized altogether, although I doubt they will ever become fully legal. Unfortunately the oscillation will continue in time and eventually lead to these substances being removed from use once more, as reactionary sentiment targets them- this next prohibition may exclude some of these substances though, as some may be adopted by various western cultures as being important for other reasons, or perhaps doctrinal, state-accepted spirituality will protect them for some time for the use of the masses.

Importantly, though, because so many of the psychotropics in use were so little known until recently, and because some grow in the wild, and because some are more generally understood to be ornamental (morning glory, san pedro cactus, and so forth) it would not be possible for any government in the world to ever truly root out all species for removal without gargantuan and tyrannical effort. Even the progressive drive towards preserving species *solely* because they are genetically unique has led to attempts to protect even dangerously powerful species. Whenever there is chocolate there will be cocaine, and whenever rye is grown there will be LSD produced.

OCCULT PHILOSOPHY

THE DIVINE ENDEAVORS AND THEIR CORRESPONDING HISTORICAL SPIRITUAL BASIS

There are various academic and social endeavors, likewise, along with psychotropics, that are important to the occult- they are either used within, or useful for elaborating on, ritualism and ceremony, or else used in psychological practices important to those who would take up occult practice. I have spoken of *sonic magick* which adapts music as ritual, and this deserves more elaboration, but it is not nearly the only form of art or academic practice that contains a cosmic element to it- it is, however, perhaps the most widely used and important, for man responds easily to music.

As with any variant of occult ceremonialism, music crafted specifically to be used for occult purposes must connect with the listener or the maker in a way such that it becomes useful for such ritualism; we would not expect to find very harsh, dark music used in a love ritual, and we would not expect very airy, light, happy music to be deployed in an effort to curse someone. What passes as "positive" or "negative" music will vary for the listener based on their own sonic preferences and their own culture; for example, someone who detests pop music will not consider the latest pop hit to be a happy song but rather to be simply annoying. Culture can overlap here as well; there are certain islamic songs used for a worshipful purpose within the middle east that are considered very relaxing and reverent there that I myself would have no such response to, because of my own inherent bias normally being directed against abrahamic practice. Similar to this, would be my response to, say, a gospel song which christians would call beautiful and which I would call an abomination of sound. I am, however, willing to admit that this is *my personal bias* and is not in any way uniform for all occultists or all humans.

OCCULT PHILOSOPHY

In the very few bits of writing and speech I have observed on the topic there appear to be two veins of occult sonic ritual- one which is purely experimental and one which appears to try and use standard psychological and visual cues to evoke a response; the latter is more dominant in occult-tinged works within mainstream music, while the former appears to be more dominant in avant-garde and experimental works you might expect to find only as a cassette in your basement. For my own work the former is far more potent but the latter is able to be broadcast to a larger audience.

I am not saying here that there is often a deliberate occult attempt being made by the music industry- actually the opposite appears to be the case and many such usages appear to mock the obsession of the abrahamists with the topic of Illuminati rituals and mind control; by deliberately inserting a few obvious occult images into a music video, the artist and the company producing the music will get a large amount of free publicity, since conspiracy websites and authors will jump on it and spread the video and accompanying song around far and wide without realizing that they themselves are the ones mainly perpetuating it. The conspiracy obsession of the modern neo-protestant revivalists has fit right in with the plans of greedy music industry producers, who make sure that every halfway decent music video contains some combination of pentagrams, pyramids, owls, fire, the eye of Horus, Satan, Jesus, blue skinned Vedic avatars, or some other mystical symbolism or figures that will give them a few million extra viewers on any such content.

Because the occult is different for different individuals the study of and practice of music will not be the same, usually, for any two occultists- nonetheless it is probably the most potent of all ritualism. I myself can almost play the keyboard and I sing as well, producing various ambient works through the mixing of sound; these low quality works actually produce more of an occult effect in my own work specifically because I tend to dwell on the darker aspects of occultism when I use my own material anyways, simply because of my own nature. I would likely not include, say, a light hearted harp solo in such materials.

OCCULT PHILOSOPHY

Music is of much greater occult importance than its use in ritualism alone; it can be used to create a mood which is more or less conducive to some specific goal or purpose, depending on the form which it takes. We expect to find specific varieties of music used in specific settings within film, for example, which when stripped of said music becomes almost completely sterile and loses virtually all of its entertainment quality as well as its ability to affect our mood. The classic "sad song" or the song that evokes images of war and carnage, or the creepy music of some B grade horror movie are all specifically designed to change the feelings of the person seeing the film, who would otherwise have little response to the material, with a few notable exceptions (the soundtrack of *The Blair Witch Project* was notably sparse, and its effect at the time notably potent.)

With music there is a process- a cycle- at play as well as within any other human field. A musical style which is seen as outdated often undergoes a schismatic tension and one "pure" core of the music remains as one or more branches emerge. We can say, for example, psychedelic rock was definitively influenced by spiritual forces (as well as, more obviously, psychotropics)- when it fractured in the late 1960s it gave birth to sub-movements; notably heavy metal, which then became its own purist genre and movement and further fractured later on. Thus we were left with a largely bubblegum-inspired psychedelic core of "pure" psychedelic, and its darker metal component, which came itself in the wake of some of the darker psychedelic forces- the band *Coven* or the works of *Iron Butterfly* can be seen as this early wave of music which carried a sort of intermediate species between psychedelic and metal works; so too did the Beatles themselves garner such works on their so-called white album with works like *Helter Skelter* which is infrequently cast as the "first heavy metal song" although this itself is just a purist argument; it is rather the first intermediate song which stretched the limits of psychedelic as the new genre emerged and took on a darker power.

OCCULT PHILOSOPHY

Writing, also, is a deeply occult art. We have to remember that in the days of old most of the population was illiterate; we must ask ourselves specifically what class of citizens living in the pre-modern era had the most ready access to learning to read and write- they were invariably of two sorts, the priestly and the occult (with the two often intertwined anyways.) The only real differentiation made here was that the priests and monks focused on historical works and religious ones while the mage or alchemist poured over mathematical and herbalist works and very often studied enough to pen their own. The lore they studied was just a counterpart in wisdom to the materials preserved by various monastic orders, but would have been considered heretical if they didn't very often pile on layers of christian rhetoric to cover up the mostly secular knowledge they were publishing and studying. From this we get a great many steganographic works which are mostly about language, mathematics, and the biological or chemical sciences, which nonetheless take the forms of grimoires which the occultist themselves knew full well had no actual spiritual basis beyond making allusions to very real spiritual figures. These deities may, from time to time, even have been included specifically to protect the knowledge in a more cosmic manner; essentially that their presence in the work allowed the same cosmic forces to protect the physical book itself.

The capability to craft one's own rituals relies on good skills with language; possibly Latin if the occultist finds it useful, but more often just a large general command of their own language. It matters little, for the purposes of the practitioner themselves, if the ritual is created in French, English, Latin, or Mandarin Chinese, and perceptions of the nature of each specific language will also be variable. Some see French, for example, as largely a language of love and frivolity and relaxation, but I see it as a language deeply engrained into the occult itself and almost inextricably bound to it in the spirit of the French Revolution and the secular and spiritual philosophies at use during that time period. It is thus, for me, actually a language of command, physical liberation, and war.

OCCULT PHILOSOPHY

Invocations penned by the occultist themselves will almost always (if they have skills crafting such work) be more potent or at least easier to make use of than those they are quite likely to stumble upon; there are hundreds of grimoires and books of spells both old and new, and many tens of thousands of shorter works containing one or a few specific rituals designed to make use of a specific force or to obtain a specific end- most often money or sex, although other things are also spoken of. Reading such works one would be led astray into the realm of nonsense, for most of these works are useless and call upon real forces only to extract unreal results, or they call upon some force or being so little understood that the concept of the original author studying them in detail from the original culture becomes laughable. The more scientific occult works- those dwelling on scientific, mathematical, and philosophical study, tend to be quite good, but those simply offering twenty pages of hexes tend to be utter hogwash and I have had many laughs reading such material.

The fact that these two groups of literature show a completely different command of the language is important to note. An occultist may have an insatiable temptation towards various academic ventures that the layperson fixating on a few lust rituals would not understand- the latter force has little capability to properly study such forces, because they do not have the command of intellect necessary to both understand them and then explain them to even a captive audience.

Writing has various oscillating styles also- none deny the power of HP Lovecraft- his works have even inspired ritual workings for various cults a century later and even a "fake" grimoire- his work contained a great deal of archaic language usage specifically to make it even darker and more foreboding. Language use is currently in its own oscillation back towards the formal, away from the informal usage which has marked the 1990s and 2000s- technology has forced a wedge between "proper" usage and the informal, and thus language is currently evolving- the formal is generally preferred within the occult, sometimes even the extreme of formal- even to the point of occasional Latin or Hindi references that aren't necessary.

OCCULT PHILOSOPHY

Art, too, carries that occult meaning- and like musical styles and writing styles, there is a cycle present in art. We see cycles and oscillations- the two are very much the same with the latter merely being more simplistic. When oscillation is present it appears to revolve more around human culture and society, whereas cosmic processes are much more convoluted because they form a much larger system.

Art chosen for a dark occult purpose will reflect this darkness and often we're left with black statues and banners with blood red inking or silver trim. Light occultism will be, obviously, brighter- up to and including the literal rainbows used by the most new age of flower child occult circles (the rainbow family comes to mind.)

Art, up until the period of Dadaism, was generally fairly formal also- realism and so forth. However, the impressionist works which had come thirty years prior were an additional component of what may be seen as a sort of anti-realism. The next wave of realism competing with anarchic art in the mid 1900s has led to the modern (technically postmodern) period in which the two have continued to fight- the two sides (arbitrarily crafted by man himself)- the realist trying to document what is, and the anarchic art forms opposite, attempting to document what can be, or is not but which the artists feel *should* be. The realist can glorify culture or cultural systems, but the anti-realist will satirize or attempt to weaken it.

Like the two serpents twining up the great occult *caduceus*, the two compete in an effort merely to differentiate so that both can be understood. I am of the mind (and this is my theory not an absolute or objective fact of any kind) that there can be no actual art without both sides existing to compete- each one casts a light evoking the shadow of the other. This somewhat vague and perhaps naïve statement will rankle a few purists on either side- the one that feels art should be "beautiful" and should never depict "ugliness" and the other that sees it solely as an expression of social activism- I'd ask the former how they arrive at objective statements of beauty and the latter how they objectively denote anything they do as activism, but I'd be doing so in vain.

OCCULT PHILOSOPHY

Speech is yet another field in which the occult finds importance- the very act of invocation requires it, and there are different modes of speech found within the occult which need to be denoted specifically- we have the hesychasm and similar tonal works, as well as the whisper (or furtive act of invoking) and the great berserker-style shouts of primal force.

Mostly though we can simply boil it down to this; that through speech understanding occurs. Therefore, the occultist must know their audience (if any) and attempt to combine speech with posture and other aspects of charisma, to truly become successful at whatever goal they desire. We must apply reason to this; will the ritual be more powerful (if it is an observed ritual) if the people therein stammer and mumble, or rather if they speak clearly and with force? Likewise, if the occultist believes some divine or demonic force is observing from some other plane, dimension, or realm, the same should be assumed to remain true. There are, of course, beings reckoned to react badly to attempts to command and would prefer a less formal act of speech and veneration.

The manner of speaking used revolves around the ritual in question, and here another cycle plays out- there are ages in which formality (and situations requiring it) is common, and ages of informality. We are, as before in a largely informal period and here growing more informal by the day- clothing and styles go right along with linguistic slang and creoles and are becoming more prevalent, with the natural backlash that growing numbers of people have grown disdainful of such things and have begun to wonder whether people's education is lacking. As before, as well, the informal and formal tone require the other to exist in order to not simply be "the way words are used." Without formality informality does not exist, and the reverse is equally true. However, as always, the two compete with one another and differentiate, splitting into thousands of different language systems and subsystems and slang terms. Education favors the formal and does a disservice in doing so- and anyone who ever studied a foreign language has learned its use in the extreme of formal and often sounds out of place in the culture using the language thus learned.

OCCULT PHILOSOPHY

There are other interesting facets here- there have been periods in which the very act of being literate in language (not just written language) was a luxury afforded only to special groups. This is the case for medieval Europe and modern day India, where lower-caste individuals often receive substandard language instruction as compared with the Brahmin class which is still innately favored despite a complete end to state-sponsored caste system reverence.

This even led to the creation of pig-latin, which is mostly a joke language used by children to communicate with clueless adults without those same adults knowing readily what is being said; this thus allows things to be said which would normally be taboo, and discussions that are unlikely to field parental approval are thus no longer off limits. Mostly we overlook such things, but we must here remember that many spoken and written systems have been created first as a form of quasi-coded speech or writing which was only readily understood by those "in the know" or part of a specific subculture- a band of thieves, an outcast minority, or perhaps rebels plotting overthrow.

I will here state that the most occult practice within human culture that can be used is one of the oldest- that of gardening and agriculture. This seems slightly out of place in the context of language and speech, art and song- purely human endeavors- however, gardening is among the oldest occupations of all, and still forms the basis of many occult ritual forms; what ritual would it be, without materials made from plants? The wand is possibly wood, the incense contains the fragrance of various plant species, the paper is organic also- so too may be the robes and hoods. Even the ritual sword may have been smithed using charcoal.

The very facet of owning a garden, in ancient cultures, was often a symbol of wealth and power- the difficulties in securing the water and soil needed for such a thing in the middle of the steppe meant that most were unable to make use of such a space.

OCCULT PHILOSOPHY

There is, quite literally, nothing more close to being a deity on this physical plane of reality, than to utterly control the location, growth, and life cycle of other living things. The Egyptians appear to have stretched this to the realm of their own feline friends, which they equally venerated, although they also had the odd habit of mummifying other creatures as well- in the modern era cat worship is more powerful than it has ever been, but anyone who has cared for such an animal knows the master and slave roles are reversed and the cat ends up being the dominant party- not so with photosynthetic life, which is immobile and will grow precisely where you put it so long as you allow it to exist- short of a killing frost the soil itself becomes a microcosm and you the deity reigning over the plot you've plowed.

In the modern pagan era much attention has been given to conservation and environmentalism; here I say that climate change is less of a risk to the world than soil degradation- we're running low on easily obtained phosphates for root crops such as the potato plant and most of the world's agricultural soils are carbon poor. Powdered charcoal added to soil restores it, when combined with compost; I've said this so far in three other literary works but it must be said here, since the occultist wishing to grow many of the herbs and plants required for their craft will need to restore the soil to do so, if it has formerly been a chemically treated lawn for decades on end, thus breaking down all organic contents and leeching the carbon out of the topsoil.

If I plant a tomato I will not reap a head of lettuce. I can utterly and completely control every aspect of my garden in as general or as micromanaged a sense as I desire and have the energy for. We might think of the insect life therein as being similar to ourselves, only that the forest of vegetables they forage in is literally controlled on every level by a far larger physical being (the occultist themselves) as to the location of resources. The ant is to a turnip plant as a human is to a redwood tree towering 100 feet over their head, with a trunk as big around as a minivan.

OCCULT PHILOSOPHY

Even gardening has experienced its cycles. There have been periods of human history where most individuals were landless peasantry, and there have been eras in which owning at least a small property was common. In Rome, after various outbreaks of fire there, it was decreed that all homes should have space between them (at least, to my knowledge, outside of the apartments and merchantile centers in certain areas of the city itself.) When we think of abrahamic spirituality we think of the Garden of Eden- with *paradise* literally taken from pagan language, which denoted an enclosed space, generally a garden, in the cultures there. When we think however of pagan gardening we're speaking of not one paradise but many- manifold gardens and groves, fields of gold and hills of green, and we think also of things such as the Hanging Gardens of Babylon, which were *not* mythical. These gardens were ostensibly constructed because the leader at the time had a wife who came from a mountainous region. Since there were no mountains they created one. This may be a latter day tale of romance from another culture, but the ruins are quite literally extant, and it appears water was brought up to a central pool on the top of this artificial mountain and garden system (built in several steps, with plants hanging from every crevice and trees in every mound) by the use of a device developed by Archimedes- a sort of hollow screw which, when turned in a liquid, would slowly draw it up the screw to a higher level continuously- several appear to have been operated in tandem, drawing fluids up to the topmost level after which runoff went down each subsequent step, irrigating the entire structure.

The combination of what was then extremely complicated engineering and science with such a thing of beauty shows the occult contrast between Eden and Babylon; the former was tended by a deity, the latter by man. The former probably didn't actually exist, but the latter still does to this day, albeit in ruins. The former was entirely natural- willed into being by a deity requiring no effort on the part of man (indeed before eating the fruit man could scarcely enjoy it, due to his possession, it is said, of a pre-human animalistic cognitive ability.) In the case of Babylon human ingenuity alone led to its construction.

OCCULT PHILOSOPHY

When man made the step from a hunter-gatherer only passively interested in the growth of other life forms (and first having supposedly domesticated cats and dogs, before laying a spade to the soil for the first time) to a true man capable of understanding the nature of agriculture on a limited basis, he effectively took control of the world around him for the first time. This is a rough mimic of the concept of artifact and ecofact within archaeology- an ecofact is a natural object manipulated and used by early humans (branches used for bedding, a simple club, etc), whereas an artifact is something bearing the hallmarks of greater human engineering. It's not unlikely that man, early on, understood that plants grew from certain other things- seeds and cuttings from existing plants- but the concept of actually conglomerating a number of these seeds or cuttings together and irrigating them, removing competitive life forms and protecting them from herbivores, was a revolutionary concept.

The very concept of modern civilization- the organized city, the temple, everything man now enjoys, all goes back to the first few agricultural remains currently understood to reside in northern Syria (although I believe agriculture dates further back and began further north than this, since the ruins at Gobekli Tepe appear to be substantial enough to have required agriculture several centuries or thousands of years before the later Syriac remains.) Man would never have had the resources necessary to construct most of what he has now had he not first developed the concept of surplus food- something the Egyptians appeared to understand and make use of regularly.

In the cycle of agriculture we appear to gravitate back and forth between naturalism and domineering; currently most food comes from mono-cultured factory farms, whether vegetable or animal in source- more and more, though, people are favoring locally and often organically grown goods- roughly equivalent to the locally grown/ locally proud mantras of the volkische movements in Central Europe during the late 1800s and into the interwar period.

OCCULT PHILOSOPHY

While the occult is the manipulation of cosmic forces, or of reality itself, agriculture and gardening is a pure form of manipulation acted out on nature itself- landscaping goes hand in hand with this facet of magick, and feng shui and other concepts would not exist were man incapable of understanding how to manipulate the wilderness around him. Rather than just gardening, landscaping should also here be mentioned separately on the basis that it doesn't always consist solely of plant life- rocks and even the choice of strata (soil) used has an effect upon the land as well, and this too changes over time as style and fashion moves ahead on its course.

We can see here one last and interesting point- the Western coast of the United States is currently in a severe drought, and well-watered lawns have fallen by the wayside in favor of arid landscaping; the use of cacti and succulents which require little if any added moisture. Man has adapted to what is now one of the worst environmental disasters of the modern age in these regions- but these small aspects of culture in these afflicted areas have not indicated a larger change in the super-culture of the region; for factories continue to dominate the area in their withdrawal of hydration for their own industrial purposes. Here there is a disconnect between the individual and the capitalistic endeavor, with regards to willingness to change day to day existence. Herein we can draw a comparison with biology, again whether divinely or naturally inspired; a simplistic life form with a shorter life and less complexity is often able to mutate more quickly than larger, more complicated forms of life, and find themselves more able to adapt to rapid change. We must remember of course that as the presumably long-lived sauropods were wiped out by (as the dominant theory states) a massive asteroid, much smaller mammalian scavengers and omnivores simply adapted at the time in response to harsher conditions, likely feasting on the carcasses of dinosaurs which had choked to death or succumbed to starvation as food sources waned.

OCCULT PHILOSOPHY

Philosophy is one of the most important of all fields within the occult which ought to be studied- here too we see (as I stated) the exchange between what might be thought of as stoicism and its brethren, and epicureanism and its own cousins.

In the now dominant age of intellect and pagan naturism, as the age of abrahamic zeal and physical force slowly wanes, there is altogether more time for philosophy in the average life- even those who study fields utterly unrelated to it end up reading the works of Plato and others- almost all fields within the humanities will at least touch on such things. This is sometimes decried within academics (or by those outside the academic world) as "fluff" with little modern importance, but nonetheless it remains a field worthy of discourse, and to relegate it to antiquity and ignore modern social philosophy is a bit humorous to those who enjoy such things.

Paracelsus is interesting as well despite being usually overlooked unless someone is majoring in philosophy as a subject of study- alchemy and herbalism here combine, and this is not the only place we see such things in even newer philosophical circles; it is virtually impossible for philosophy to separate itself from the spiritual, and even secular, or outright atheistic, philosophies mention spirituality, if only to condemn them- here is another oscillation and another dichotomy; the secular philosophies would have no such label if there was no spiritual philosophy to decry and the reverse as well occurs. Likewise, the two "sides" struggle as any other. Only a century ago most intellectuals still said that morality ultimately came from above- now most of the intellectuals of the world say it is subjective and comes from man's mind. We need not choose a side, because occultism is compatible with both; yet at the same time we have to regard the interplay between subjectivity and objectivity in order to make use of such things.

OCCULT PHILOSOPHY

It can be explained in brief, at least as to my own feelings on the subject; many philosophical and spiritual systems claim objectivity for their beliefs- the christian (religious christians, anyways) will claim that their morality comes from their god- thus, it is objectively true, because their deity is all powerful and controls the very concept of morality. Normally, this claim is followed by allusions to the same being existing outside of the laws he created (or which "it" created) thus exempting it from various paradoxical situations such as the paradox *"can god create a stone so heavy he cannot lift it?"*

The claim of objectivity is true in some cases- when we say that something pertains to anthropic terms only and explanations of the world- that is, it exists only within man's understanding- we can say the statement is objectively true, but herein lies a caveat- it is only objectively true within man's subjective understanding. If I state that the sky is blue, that claim is true- the sky is indeed that specific shade of color (at least if the sky is clear.) However, the very terms I use here are only valid within man's understanding and situation; making the same statement on Mars would be objectively false, perhaps, and the sky would actually be yellow.

This is to say; a claim or statement can be *objectively* and absolutely true only insofar as it deals solely with observable, anthropic situations- everywhere else, the claim of objectivity is itself subjective and normally based on some combination of false assumption (*"the bible is true because god says so, and he says so in the bible"*) or misconstruing our own understanding of reality as the only one which holds validity- which may itself be utterly wrong, if some theoretical physicists' hypotheses are correct. We may of course be living in some vast illusion, or perhaps our concept of time is completely falsified in other dimensions. Nonetheless, an objective claim can be made, insofar as it pertains to descriptions which contain only human experience; concepts such as divinity, morality, and so forth, cannot be objective, unless assumptions are made- this is not to say that they are necessarily *wrong* although I can formulate an opinion that they are indeed not factual; I merely say they cannot be presumed to be objective in any (amusingly) objective sense.

OCCULT PHILOSOPHY

History is yet another study of great importance within the occult- and this is true for a variety of reasons. We have all heard it said, that those who do not learn from history are doomed to repeat it; this somewhat vague moral lesson is nonetheless at least sensible within the study of the occult, since we can look back at several thousand years of well documented ritualism and find examples of its change over time in accordance with the process of spiritual evolution. Perhaps the occult, based on experimentation, has survived so easily precisely because it is able to change rather than clinging to antiquated dogma, even though some modern purists try to make it do so.

The interaction between history and those who lived it, as well as those who came after history was made and how it affected them, is all worthy of consideration, and it is solely through reviewing history that we can find the patterns of oscillation and cycling present therein and draw conclusions about the present as well as predict the near future and, at times, further into the future as well. If one could perfectly comprehend history without bias, they would likely be taken by most to be clairvoyant.

That, though, is the rub- history is almost always and almost fated to be biased in its presence; we look at something as (relatively) recent as the American Civil War and say that modern beliefs on the subject vary according to those who procure and perpetuate documentation thereof- the reasons for the war, for each loss or victory, for each leader's perceived weakness or strength, will vary depending on who is asked to make a statement about such things. A sympathetic new wave Confederate will likely postulate about these things and come to a widely different conclusion than a historian from a northern region who works at preserving Yankee artifacts from the period. So, too, would we expect variable opinions and inherently biased statements on any other subject where the events or people or places were subject to man's opinion. I regard archaeology as the purest form of history- literally history regarding extant physical remains; although here also most knowledge gleaned is relative to established knowledge or else is purely theorized about.

OCCULT PHILOSOPHY

We understand the world in terms of comparing new phenomena with established ones, so if the basis of our knowledge of the old is flawed, so too will be our knowledge of the new. Look to Crete for an example of this facet of history and its problems- the civilization there almost surely has nothing to do with the antiquated tale of King Minos, yet the remains there (which may be connected to those at Santorini) were postulated to be such by Arthur Evans when excavations began there- in reality the culture there was merely an extraordinarily sophisticated one about which little else is known other than that their engineering skills were, at the time (during the bronze age) unmatched in scope- the Greek cultures of the Aegean were still living in single floor buildings at the time and here was a palace containing upwards of 1,300 rooms with a wall structure capable of withstanding major earthquakes. The surrounding city could have held several tens of thousands of people- quite a feat for the era- and must have been the most extravagant of places for wealth and power at the time, possibly even forming the basis of the myth of Atlantis; regardless though, the culture there was probably not itself Minoan, although the label has stuck and in retrospect this is now the term used.

World War Two is much the same; here there is a more potent change between biased accounts. For some decades following the war it was a sort of common knowledge reality that Hitler and the Nazis were pure evil and desired world domination. In the last decade or thereabouts discourse has switched somewhat and it is now more generally accepted that the Nazi party never had designs for world conquest and were predominantly concerned with destroying the Soviets and grabbing up only as much of Western Europe as they held prior to the Treaty of Versailles. It certainly seems that a great many statist politicians and pro-Israeli activists want to criminalize saying such things as a form of "antisemitism"- interesting since restrictions on speech and expression were the stereotypical hallmarks of every claim about the Third Reich. In the future this trend may continue, or it may reverse and Hitler will end his reign as comedian in chief (for he has largely become a satirical figure in the last twenty years- one to be chuckled at) and begin anew a reign as Satan incarnate.

OCCULT PHILOSOPHY

The occultist should reject such biased accounts and attempt to glean the purest possible truth if they wish to use historical records and theories as a basis for understanding the nature of reality or to predict future movements. Many people presume that time periods repeat- they're saying this now and comparing our current era with the early 1990s on the basis that two of the candidates likely running for the US presidency are from respectively the Bush and Clinton families, and that "gas prices are low." This overlooks the situation elsewhere in the world which has little in common with the 1990s- during that era there was (relative) peace in Europe and a great deal of economic cooperation, but in this current period there is relative struggle and paranoia, a greater deal of general religious violence, and general economic collapse in Asia and Europe.

Thus, those making such a comparison have done so only by looking at a few rather small aspects of fairly recent history without an eye to older historical trends or to other aspects of culture. I have stated to others that we are not in a repeating 1990s era cycle right now, so much as a period roughly similar to the 1930s. All the hallmarks are there- we've had a major power get defeated and hemorrhage land (formerly Germany, now the USSR-turned-Russia) we have rising nationalism in Europe and elsewhere, we have numerous border disputes in Asia (formerly colonial lands, now sovereign) we have a focus on energy resources; formerly one of the major lead-ups to Hitler's North African movements, just as the colonial powers cracked the Ottoman Empire apart, leading to the Turks remaining neutral and granting the Germans free movement. We even have styles right now reminiscent of the late flapper era, if you look hard enough. I remember some years ago seeing a new line of dresses and remarking that they looked like the sort of things worn in the depression-era photographs my grandfather had. So too do we have cultural paranoia and anarchism prevalent in Europe and elsewhere; people have become disenfranchised and are splitting into those who wish to smash the system, and those who adopt racially volkische motives. It is not possible to predict the future, but I can say with fair certainty that if world diplomacy does not extinguish the rising tide of distrust and fear currently gripping the world, that dark times *are* ahead in the coming decade or so.

OCCULT PHILOSOPHY

When I say world diplomacy I of course mean the reform of top-heavy government, rather than governments cracking down on those expressing such fear, disdain, and outright hatefulness- if the latter occurs then I would be ready to predict for certain that dark times are ahead, while the former could break the cycle altogether, if what I am observing is a repeat of the interwar period and not just some randomized cosmic aberration.

Those wishing to understand not the *certain* future (which relies upon belief in determinism and a finite system in which all component cycles can theoretically be documented and known) but rather the *likely* future should look to history. Find correlations between current events and ancient ones, especially where multiple paths overlap- the main paths of concern for such work are all within the realm of humanity because man himself has innate biological and cultural cycles as such beings interact with one another; in fact these cycles would probably be far more easily seen were it not for the influence of cosmic movements. If an occultist should find that there are five or six major correlations between current events and those from the past they can attempt to use this situation as a predictor of future actions- modernizing those, of course, in accordance with the existence of totally new philosophies, spiritual groups, or technologies which may not have existed formerly. When I say I believe we are repeating the 1930s interwar period, I don't mean that we will see another Third Reich, or that man is about to plunge headlong into World War Three (likely wiping himself out in the process)- rather I say that international frustration is likely to ensue and cooperation likely to break down, as the world becomes increasingly in competition for limited energy reserves. In the new era, this has taken the form of an increasingly frenetic east trying to outmaneuver NATO with both sides suffering severe cultural malaise as world trade breaks down traditional societal beliefs and structures.

OCCULT PHILOSOPHY

The final system to be considered here is that of mathematics. If we assume that the cosmos are deterministic then everything can be quantified in mathematical terms, and we would not expect, given past evidence, to see any of our physical laws here in this universe broken, because doing so would be, if not impossible, at least extraordinarily difficult and well beyond our relatively primitive attempts.

If we assume though that the cosmos are not deterministic but rather limitless, mathematics *does not* in any way lose its value for occult purposes; it merely loses objectivity, and becomes what I and others believe it to be- a finite system by which we understand finite components of a far larger, limitless system. Regardless, mathematics has done more for this world than almost any other field of study, affecting architecture, chemistry, medicine, and all other fields.

Numbers themselves can carry occult symbolism; however the purer form of occultism here with some of those notions can actually be less important than its use within more mainstream works- a working knowledge of at least intermediate mathematical principles is intrinsic to the types of calculations likely to be made regarding any magickal ceremonialism- at the very least the movement of some of the more important celestial bodies, and so forth.

Some have become obsessed with numbering systems which themselves revolve only around the most basic math- such as previously mentioned systems where any number above 9 is simply broken down and its digits added together, then further reduced if need be until a number from 1 through 9 remains- this is extremely simple, such that a first grader could, with a day's practice, master the technique.

It is, rather, preferable that an occultist should study mathematics where possible, regardless of whether the systems they study have any spiritual connotations whatsoever- and chaos theory is perhaps the most interesting of the mathematical concepts outside of the occult, strictly speaking- and, interestingly, perhaps the one at play the most when predictions are attempted.

OCCULT PHILOSOPHY

ONE GOD MANY EXPRESSIONS: ONE LIFE MANY DIVERGENT FORMS

There is an important correlation here to state- one which cannot be overlooked and must be mentioned; that of, once again, the correlation between the human conception of the divine (in some cultures and spiritual circles) and the observable physical reality around us.

When I speak of all life on this planet belonging to diverged forms of one primordial life form (thus making all life essentially the same, and differentiated in response to often non-biological stimuli) I can compare this with certain beliefs regarding sacred figures. In eastern paths, there is commonly the belief that there is one essential divine creative force, and that the various deities described by religions and spiritual systems are essentially divergent forms of the same one divine force- such is the case in Vedic lore, where we have figures such as Brahma and Vishnu and Shiva each representing not a truly sovereign being but rather an expression of the one force behind them all, which is roughly equivalent to how a monotheist would refer to their one deity.

That is, the difference between east and west is less about polytheism versus monotheism, but rather that the former diverges their *one* omnipotent force into different aspects, both to explain them and to weave mythology, whereas the latter recognizes just one deity which adopts all forms simultaneously- however this supposedly monotheistic abrahamic force is attended by various angelic beings which themselves are immortal or nearly so and possess various powers of a spiritual and sometimes physical nature- how then can this be truly monotheism? And why is it that this one being posited by abrahamism seems to lack true omnipotence, being unable, for example, to lie or to go back on his or it's own word? Surely, a being possessed of limitless capability would have little reason to regard mankind as important enough to swear vows to- and surely this being could occasionally break its own rules for amusement or to teach some cautionary lesson.

OCCULT PHILOSOPHY

We see here the three aspects of the biological world; we have three corresponding values, which can be spoken of.

The monotheistic beliefs (of the west) represent the aspect of life as singular; the single divine source from which life began, or the single life form from which all others later stemmed from. Their one high creator is undifferentiated and limited- perhaps the desire not to have such limitations, could be said to be the basis for this differentiation- the ability to experience through the use of multiple competing, interacting physical forms.

The polytheistic beliefs (specifically those of the pagans) represent the divergent aspect of life- the recognition that while these forms came from one source, they are nonetheless now, at least on the physical level, sentient beings which think of themselves as separate. They are limited, just as the true pantheons contained deities which had certain, but not all, powers.

The polytheistic aspect of the east represents the period in between these two fields; The beings are divergent, but still connected to that one divine, cosmic force- they are separate in form and sometimes in will, but yet they all share the same general nature of their power.

Through recognizing this we can make two major statements; the first and more important that *the physical reality around us correlates to these spiritual archetypes.* With the second and less important being *Spiritual forms created by mankind correlated to innate biological principles which he observed around him over time, even when he lacked the ability to fully quantify them.*

This is to say, there is worth within all spiritual paths so long as the occultist is able to understand their nature. This can be difficult, for those locked into one particular path in which they spiritually exclude the others from all acknowledgment. I can thus say that, while some spiritual forms bring more joy or more pain to the world, they all have correspondences to be noted nonetheless.

OCCULT PHILOSOPHY

Even the very aspect of a "good" or "bad" spiritual belief here is to be noted as well, because the positive aspect of existence is only seen in relation to that which is negative. This is why, with all spiritual systems, there is some sort of divine energy, and some form of demonic or negative energy that goes hand in hand with it- there could quite literally be no god in christiandom without Satan, because without Satan there is no reason to regard worship or veneration of the deity as important- were it not for the fear of Hell most people would have abandoned such practices long ago and embraced outright hedonism.

The fact that dishonest religious orders tell their followers that it is necessary to adopt strict ascetic practices (almost always related to consumption of food and drink, as well as to sexual practices and money) shows that they only comprehend one side of this spiritual system- the Buddhist, in this way, is just as far behind in their development as any Christian, and both are as held back and delusional as a complete barbarian who believes indulgence alone is good. Oddly, within almost all of these spiritual orders, this asceticism levied against the laypeople does not extend to the clergy, which lives a sheltered existence, often filled with riches, on the backs of those doing actual work. The very notion that a spiritual school, empowered by a deity, even needs monetary support is laughably wrong; if their deity or their pantheon has such power they have no need for the support of fallible mortals with their coins.

The fact that the biological appears to so closely approximate the divine (at least natures of the divine in this manner) shows us that there is some sort of cosmic design- this does not necessarily indicate theism; if a spiritualist with no gods feels that these forces are innate or extra-dimensional, so be it. Some might be tempted to say that it is because of this innate *biological* feature that those same divine philosophies arose- I find it difficult to believe that primitive man, ten thousand years ago or more, had enough understanding of his own biology and that of other creatures to develop such a concept. Let alone, that the first systems appear to have crafted the deified on a biological basis that goes beyond merely "here is the snake god, represented by a snake."

OCCULT PHILOSOPHY

We might variously regard the figures venerated by man as being impure representations of beings which exist on some other plane, as well, and which are merely capable of manifesting in this one either through accident or will- we might imagine that we, in our day-to-day thoughts, might project a vision of ourselves into lower dimensions where we also exist- in which case we might imagine there are cults based on aspects of each of us in those same realms. It's an interesting idea, that life forms which regard us as infinitely existing and untouchable and intangible might be worshiping our own imaginations, which nonetheless on their plane of reality have become physically manifested.

Or, we might presume that man's representation of such forces is actually pure and real and that these beings are actually conscious and literally extant- that they have some further design in acting upon our world. We then need to consider, what exactly it is that they could possibly want, if anything, and why specifically they are interested in our seemingly mundane world.

For, speaking both in spiritual and secular terms, our world and its inhabitants must be presumed to be relatively mundane- it is mathematically just shy of impossible that there isn't other advanced life in existence on our very observable third dimensional plane, and there is nothing in any reasonable spiritual path which precludes the existence of extra-terrestrial life forms themselves possessed of an understanding of spiritual and technological concepts. When we regard this as true, a lot of the egotism of our own spiritual systems begins to lose credibility, because much of it refers only to man as a special or unique creation of some cosmic being, and never goes into any detail regarding other life forms- unless we regard the tales of Annunaki as being similar enough to those of star people or angels and say they are the same thing- that the higher force in turn spawned lower forces which to us seemed as deities but were actually life forms separate from ourselves and our world.

OCCULT PHILOSOPHY

FREEDOM IS ULTIMATELY THE HIGHEST TRUTH

Under the concept of spiritual evolution, it is plain that the process of evolution is at action; this occurs on a cultural basis as well, and the two intertwine. Since this process is largely preferable to stagnation, and because it is innate, we have to observe that there are certain facets of the sovereign man which lend themselves well to this process continuing.

The most important of all of these is liberty itself; it may not be possible to break the cycle alluded to (imperfectly) in *Republic* where a cycle of timocracy, democracy, oligarchy, and tyranny is expounded upon by Plato, but where liberty is greatest, there we see the greatest improvement over time in a culture- we can correlate this with biology. A colony containing many billions of bacteria will be more resistant to negative stimuli than one in which far fewer are present, because the chance that some of them will be immune to the detrimental stimuli is greater when their numbers are so- likewise, where the greater mass of people is capable of choice and advancement and progress, this society will naturally be healthier than a society in which decisions are predominantly made by a small body of empowered individuals, who as an aggregate total are less likely to formulate appropriate ideas and reactions to culture and society, let alone to any biological or cosmic process.

Here the value of the revolutionary period is seen again, as it was expounded that all citizens had certain rights which were inviolable; these individuals- both in France and the United States as well as other cultures thereafter- appear to have been involved directly with occult philosophy, for many were Masons and many were surely aware of works dating to the same period speaking about what was then fringe science. The devised system, the grand design crafted by this period, was one in which mankind was strengthened by the recognition that there was no intrinsic master and servant beyond the divine realm, and that this too was to remain malleable and separate from what they envisioned as secular, extremely limited government. We have largely forsaken this concept and have mostly reaped pain for doing so.

OCCULT PHILOSOPHY

It does not matter if there is a "true" spiritual path to the exclusion of others. Each individual within such a path ought only to ask one thing; which is, "If my path is true, and obviously so, and my deity all powerful, why should I need to expound its principles through a governing body, when the deity and spiritual path are so much higher?" To do so, to assume an omnipotent being and then to try and "help" it would be a denigration of the power of that same being, highly insulting in nature, and would be akin to determining that the Amazon needed help flowing, and to dump a single bucket of water into it, thinking this a fruitful endeavor.

In reality the most denigrating thing a practitioner or believer in any cosmic force can do is to presume that it requires a helping hand beyond emulating the characteristics of that god or force- the messiah of the christians frequently told his followers to adopt an ascetic lifestyle and wander to and fro owning little or no material wealth, yet we observe the mega church with its golden domes and silver crosses and thousand dollar suits- it is difficult to reconcile these two separate visions of the spiritual system together. We see the same thing in many spiritual circles, and yet all of these organized groups tend to adopt the same practice; to limit the spiritual workings of the laity with fair regularity.

What does it say about a spiritual "leader" who thinks his or her own path so lacking in potency that they must constantly attempt to manipulate or influence their followers? What does it say about a governing body or system which uses force as the predominant method of keeping the peace? The two are equivalent; in both cases the distrust of the capability of the laypeople or citizens is combined with disdain for those outside of some upper hierarchy, and this combination is usually lethal, eventually collapsing the religion or state on the same basis because the process of cultural or spiritual advancement has been slowed to a crawl and beliefs and practices have become static. Unable to change for the better, such beliefs and practices eventually strangle the religion or state by binding it to workings which lack further use.

OCCULT PHILOSOPHY

Likewise the concept of liberty is held within the occult itself- purism aside a great deal of experimentation takes place regardless of stringency and strictures developed by more organized orders. I would submit here that most such orders at best are offering a very small piece of occult or spiritual knowledge while withholding most of it, and even outright forbidding or attempting to prohibit a proactive search for additional educational attainment on spiritual topics. As I stated, this is at least part of the reason for the prohibition of psychotropic substances that came in the wake of temperance era moralism.

Liberty is a *necessity* within the spiritual. It is likewise a necessity within the physical. A person is incapable of purifying their own spiritual state unless they are free to make mistakes or "bad" decisions. A person is incapable of advancing technology or learning or culture itself without being capable of experimenting and risking a less than favorable outcome. If we assume divine compulsion- determinism, or something of that ilk- is true, then the spiritual should be forsaken altogether because it is not possible to make one's own decisions outside of fate. If this is the case, it's a sad state to exist within, and freedom itself becomes an illusion unable to be objectively used.

Every facet of modern spirituality has come into existence because someone broke away from former paths and beliefs and developed a path or belief that was new- it may have incorporated pieces of older paths or beliefs but it has a new label, and often new practices and usage. To limit spirituality or society through the use of compulsion (usually crafted by a government or church although it can take the form of simple societal shunning of fringe ideas) is to starve it of new blood, and to deny the very existence of evolution outside of the biological- but it is precisely this evolutionary biological model that is emulated by all dynamic, healthy spiritual and national bodies. That which works is retained, that which does not is archived and falls into disuse for another period where it may once again have some sort of usefulness. Thus the occult must not seek to destroy any aspect of belief but to challenge the old and formulate the new, driving progress in a calculated direction, but not considering its findings to be static and unchanging.

OCCULT PHILOSOPHY

In the most odd twist of fate, those forces which exert the most control over a body of citizens or congregants are the most misled, the most likely to be wrong about other topics, and the least likely, in time, to continue surviving. Their ferocious tenacity is completely offset by the innate desire of both their members and detractors to be free to make their own decisions, and this force, when suppressed, eventually emerges with even more vibrancy than when it began. At some point, this demolishes the older system entirely and often the liberating belief becomes suppressive towards the old- which creates a situation nearly as bad as before. Today's revolutionary, thus, becomes tomorrow's tyrant; just as a new spiritual form which liberates people from the former when it suppressed change, can later in turn become the tyrant itself, and begin actively oppressing those who hold to any of those older tenets, even if their own version has been substantially changed. This is a risk that is run any time a charismatic spiritual head or head of state comes into power, and it's a risk run every time a new spiritual group that was once small and meaningless manages to first become a tolerated minority, and then rise up through the ranks from a fringe religious body, to a mainstream religious order, to a dominant cultural force.

The human mind, in its confused state regarding death especially, and the meaning of life (for life and death are paired enigmatic concepts) seeks knowledge- it seeks answers. In a strange juxtaposition of claim and reality, the same orders offering them the most definitive answers, claimed as objective fact and based on divine inspiration, are the least healthy orders of all; rather these same groups should tell their followers to question and think and enjoy freedom, and spend their lives partly devoted not to listening to self appointed leaders expound truth, but rather to seek it for themselves. It is through this singular process; the very act of critical thought, that purer and purer truth is found. Perhaps, there is *no* truth and merely situational reality; in which case the same concept is still the highest- if there is truth, it should be sought by as many people as possible. If there is only subjective bias and opinion, the largest plurality of such beliefs should be expounded and interacted with one another to form systems and spiritual paths which work at least for specific eras.

OCCULT PHILOSOPHY

CARE FOR NATURE MUST REFLECT ANY DIVINE CARE FOR US

The natural world contains a great deal of biology within it- as such protecting these biomes and lands is of importance as well. The human is sentient and sovereign; able to judge, able to imagine and predict, able to use his advanced understanding to quantify the world. What worse a way is there to react to this capability, than to dirty our own metaphoric human nest and destroy it?

Many humans are worried about, for example, some cosmic catastrophe ending our world- a gigantic asteroid, or apocalyptic celestial explosion, or maybe an invasion by hostile aliens. In the face of this fear, though, humans persist at destroying the very same world they already enjoy and inhabit, through the wanton raping of natural resources- even political and societal theories supposedly developed to improve the situation usually do the same thing. The same collectivism that was supposed to ensure a pastoral, tolerable, peaceful life for easterners circa the age of Lenin ended up instead leading to the development of industry and weaponry that polluted entire regions- there are lakes in this world that are more chemical than water, and there are fields and hills so radioactive that inhabitants living too close end up with eight toes and four ears on their legs.

Humans are a unique case, at least for this planet- we're a part of nature and a biological life form as any other, yet we imagine ourselves as separate from it. Even those that comprehend the need for protecting nature usually speak of "our responsibility" in such a manner that one would imagine they deny our biological nature- we are merely the most "intelligent" of the many divergent life forms that sprung forth from one source on this one single planet, with quite likely millions of other such sentient races in the cosmos- this was understood to be true by those who bothered to think about the mathematics behind even just our galaxy, for it too is vast- so vast that we might very well imagine it to be teeming with life, regardless of the universe at large.

OCCULT PHILOSOPHY

If all of the trees are cut, there will be no wood fire for ceremonial workings, no charcoal for incense- if the soil degrades and becomes sterile we will have no herbs for our rituals, and without the animals, where would even the darkest, most chaotic occultist acquire the bones they may need for some work of evil? From the most light hearted white magician to the most icy black sorcerer or mage, we all rely on nature to supply us.

"As above, so below"- the cosmos recycles material into itself over and over again and renews it (renewal here being purely a human concept.) If a star explodes, all of that material flying off in every direction will, in the long span of time, end up absorbed into some other star, or hit a planet, or perhaps even an asteroid. Not one particle is truly wasted in this process, and the cosmos, in its vast wonderment, is beautiful. I assure everyone, that intelligent life exists elsewhere; let us hope it acknowledges this divine cycle and has based its belief systems upon it.

The world itself is the only body we currently occupy. If we as a sentient race inhabited a few dozen planets scattered around a few star systems we might be able to occasionally rip one of these same bodies apart to extract massive amounts of resources without worrying about the consequences- but since we have one world only, we will go extinct if we abuse it too heavily. Some cynics believe this to be a good thing, and they come in two variants; first, those disdainful of humanity as a whole upon observing its many faults, and those secondly that are so purely dark in their beliefs that they wish nothing but suffering.

Many occultists have pets- cats and snakes may be rather a stereotype in this case but they seem to be popular nonetheless. I have never known an occultist to randomly abuse and kill their pet- then why do we as a race randomly abuse and attempt to kill our entire planet? Here is truth- there is no need for a Satan, when man fulfills that stereotypical role himself with great effectiveness. Even things which ought to be positive- technology and cultural advancement, and so forth- are then applied to nature and used to degrade it. One might think that darker minds perhaps want us all to forget that we come from forests, plains, and sea shores unspoiled by any industry.

OCCULT PHILOSOPHY

The occult has its roots in the pastoral; this has been partly forgotten in modernity because more and more occult work takes place in the realm of technology. Rather, the two should combine, and the practitioner *must* dedicate themselves towards the protection of nature, even if it involves only their own property, or a single flower pot.

With power comes responsibility- if the occultist believes he or she has acquired power, whether it be through the means of rudimentary reason, or spiritual communication, then this should be dedicated towards action. It is not enough to simply say we must protect the world, it is more important to use our capabilities to do so. If you are in league with Lucifer, you are conjoined to a cosmic force which could not possibly support the pillaging of this planet, which results in the exclusion of liberty and the necessity of servitude force-fed to a famine stricken population by a few oligarchs who siphon most goods for themselves.

Man in his current, egotistical form, is more a parasite than an animal; through our consoling delusions we have convinced ourselves that we are so important that no force can destroy us; but another truth is this; that even if no "natural" force can do so, *we* are able to destroy *ourselves*. Our capability to overcome otherwise natural forces and defend against them is meaningless when the force causing the destruction is our own hand. We might imagine that we, in our current state, are like a lunatic who attempts to choke himself to death with one fist while holding it back with the other hand- a foolish errand which benefits nobody. This planet is ailing, specifically because we have decided that nothing is above our own temporal amusement and temporary diversion.

This shows lack of foresight more than anything. Man has already wiped out species before that he found useful for enjoyment. The dodo bird was killed off fairly quickly, specifically because it had not been predated upon and could be approached at will and carried off for eating. This one example is weak, though, since it is also an example of the purification of world genetics- the species would also have died off eventually had some predatory animal from non-human nature found itself in the same region.

OCCULT PHILOSOPHY

Sadly some believe that if the world begins to fall, some god or cosmic force will finally show itself and help our race, or redeem its followers to the exclusion of most of man (which then, in such tales, is usually sent to some fiery chasm of hate for eternity.) This delusional belief is the ultimate cause of much of man's stupidity- a person who believes the world will eventually be destroyed for cosmic purposes anyways and subsequently rebuilt for the use of all (or a select few) has no reason to conserve, no reason to care about a world which will be decimated anyways and come back much improved.

It is much the same with such egotistical beliefs and human activity towards itself as well; much of the fighting and war from past eras has either been caused by, or encouraged by, his religions, or else the fighting began and the priestly class quickly defined it as some holy struggle of great value and integrity, with its warriors as zealous and pious templars on the battlefield opposing some evil force.

In the days of old when people were more generally connected to nature (which they were surrounded by constantly) they understood, or at least had some grasp, of a greater spiritual world in which they played but one role, and that the sentience and intelligence they enjoyed were not meant to be misused. They comprehended the concept of interconnected nature. Only the fact that more warlike people eventually displaced, destroyed, or otherwise forced them out allowed the wholesale slaughter of nature to take place. In one manner, this was not without its benefits- these groups ended up adopting some of those same naturist beliefs in time, and we see a major resurgence of it now as well, even if it is politicized and partially misses the mark. Regardless, without this one single world our entire race will be destroyed, as it currently cannot inhabit any other body. If we do find a habitable planet within reach this may change, but for now we are a one-world species, not a multi-world species as we eventually may be- and we never will be unless we persist here and continue to advance over time.

OCCULT PHILOSOPHY

IF THE EGO IS UNIQUE WE PERSIST. IF THE EGO IS NOT UNIQUE WE PERSIST. DEATH IS AN ILLUSION

In all ventures the occultist must realize that there is a strange paradox which is both enjoyable and frustrating. For thousands of years, man has sought some avenue to immortality, some way to prevent himself from succumbing to decay and being recycled into other biological matter. Truly, with modern technology it is perhaps possible to extend a person's life well beyond the natural- perhaps even forever, although such a process would be costly and likely available only to the wealthy; I am sure some of them actively encourage and fund such research. This has its own moral problems which it will surely spawn, although I predict this will be quickly fixed by the will of the masses, when it becomes clear to those that make a living guarding the rich that they are not reaping the benefit of immortality themselves.

The paradox is this; so long as man is concerned predominantly with his own ego, any attempt to attain immortality is fruitless, because the conception he holds of immortality is a false conception and refers only to the physical body, which is fated eventually to decay or be destroyed; even if his life span was limitless, it would not make him invulnerable and he would eventually find himself killed through some exterior process. However, if a person refers to the spiritual, to the *true* occult path, immortality is not possible, it is assured; the ego itself will change form and be transmuted upon death in accordance with all cycles.

If a bacterium dies, other life will feed upon it and absorb its biological tissues. The same is true with any life form which passes beyond volition and begins to decay. If a solar system "dies" the star at the center, or a black hole, or some other body will eventually absorb every particle of cold, dead matter. The larger the system, the longer it takes to be transmuted because of the physical laws present here in this realm.

OCCULT PHILOSOPHY

The human is biologically no larger than most other developed, convoluted life on the planet and, if a human corpse is left alone for some time without preservation, will very swiftly decay into nothing more than a discolored skeleton. Considering the ego, it is of course not a physical thing in the same sense, and it will take longer to transmute specifically because it continues to persist elsewhere.

Nothing is destroyed but merely changes form; the same scientists that embrace the laws of conservation seem unable to apply them to the spiritual, partly because so many mainstream religions posit a physical resurrection and spend most of their time discussing subjective law and sin. Rather, it fits to make simply the statement that *we persist* regardless of whether the ego is unique. I must explain the reasoning here.

If the ego is a unique thing, it will persist, because the ego must have thus been fated to come into existence (or perhaps always did) and either has a divine force or source behind its existence, or else is unique in that it ties us to other dimensions in which biological decay is meaningless. If the ego is *not* unique then we may just as well think of it as a robotic function created by neural awareness; a sort of self-illusion spawned by the brain. If the latter is the case, it matters little, since it means that when the ego or brain functions also decay into blackness, there is no uniqueness and therefore nothing keeping "you" from merely jumping to another body- since egos thus would all be technically homogenous or outright illusory. If the ego is more a mechanism than a divine thing, then it is perfectly plausible that one of several things would logically happen- you would repeat your life over and over (probably in slightly different form each time acknowledging string theory) or else because all matter is linked in these higher dimensions, you would proceed to experience a number of lives, occasionally with your biological material being non-biological for periods that, nonetheless, you would be unawares of and thus these spans of time however long would seem to pass in seconds.

OCCULT PHILOSOPHY

I say, that immortality is real, and we have already achieved it, because there is no process by which I can imagine the human ego can be destroyed- if of course I believe in science as I do. Since we are immortal, most of the subjective laws man has ever made can be classed in several categories; subjective laws nonetheless good because they serve a pragmatic purpose, subjective laws that are not necessary and get in the way of enjoyment, and logically or philosophically derived truth based on some mixture of occult belief and theoretical science. In all cases, *all* such regulations of human behavior are by default subjective and subject to change- this means any law or moral code which seems to lack pragmatism and cause more harm than good should be abandoned if possible and all people should attempt to enforce such views on their representation, whatever it may be.

We should here consider the possible natures of divinity as well since they are so intrinsically tied to man's conception of the spiritual. If a person makes the claim that a singular, invisible being in the skies watches everything in creation but shows a remarkably anthropocentric proclivity towards caring only about the human race and their dietary choices and ritual practices, I find such a claim hard to entertain. If, however, the monotheist posits that this divine force is agendered and sentient but concerned with all order, that is a theory that, however much I disagree with it, can at least be entertained. Likewise, it could be that all the deities we regard are some sort of energetic pantheon or perhaps the result of extra-terrestrial visitation. This latter concept matters little with regards to immortality, unless we wish to discuss figures like Pluto at great length.

It is also possible there is no actual divine force behind the cosmos and we witness order only because it mathematically arose and is innate- this is a hard concept for some to swallow, but makes just as much sense. Or, reality as we know it could entirely be an illusion of some sort- an artificial reality covering the real existence like a veil, in which case science and the occult may amusingly, eventually find themselves both trying to peel the same veil back to reveal truth.

OCCULT PHILOSOPHY

Man, in his early and dim understanding of the world, naturally feared death. How horrific it must have been, when the village elder suddenly fell on his side and worms began devouring his body. A thousand demonic entities must, after all, have been posited as the cause- thousands of years ago Neanderthals already buried the dead, and this practice could have revolved either around not wanting to see the decomposition because it was morbid, or because they felt that somehow it would prevent the person from dying in a spiritual sense. If the latter is true, we have little evidence that man at this time (for Neanderthals were closer to most modern human culture than other hominids and was the truest "human" at the time) had more than a very small set of spiritual practices and beliefs. He must have understood the concept of mortality, and the psychedelics he was surely imbibing likely gave him guidance as to how to prevent the death of the true self- the ego- even as the physical body began to decay.

Many oppose the concept of reincarnation on the basis that the number of life forms on the planet was once quite small and has grown over time- they say thus that souls are created, or that the theory itself is hokum. If the cosmos is limitless, then any increase of life in one area corresponds to a loss of it somewhere else, such that there is balance- but even this is not strictly true, for a limitless realm contains limitless life even if most of the celestial bodies are uninhabited, for the infinite value therein is indivisible.

Nonetheless, reincarnation is a physical reality- the manner of its scope and function is more difficult to discern, since so far nobody has (truly) come back from the dead- it is not a sane belief, to say that a person can truly die, and then return; if they were truly, fully dead their body would have decayed and even if they were revived the organic damage to their tissues would be so great that they would very quickly succumb to organ failure or blood poisoning or one of a host of other ills. As well, their brain would have begun to decay- beyond the usual loss of memory or lowered cognitive function usually ascribed to "near death" experiences. That term is key- the person was near death, but not actually dead, and many a charlatan has misused their experience to reap monetary rewards.

OCCULT PHILOSOPHY

VIBRATION: THE DIMENSION AS A RADIO STATION

Those who began to refer to existence as a sort of radio station were at first considered to be amusing heretics by science, until theoretical physics gained dominance and (often aided by psychedelics used by scientists themselves) expanded upon our view of reality as a race of beings. Indeed, all we have to do is presume this very possible theory, for a moment, to be true, in order to see how it could result in all manner of occult and paranormal phenomena; if our existence is simply a form of elongated vibrating energy, mostly empty save for those same vibrating forms, then our reality could utterly overlap in the same dimensional plane with many others, each one merely at a different frequency. If this is the case, then we might regard phenomena of an unexplainable nature to be interference, and the occult as the willful or accidental manipulation of the same.

Interesting things can be done with electronics- not just with radios. Magnetic anomalies were one of Tesla's many loves, and form at least a part of paranormal research; hold a magnet to the antennae of a radio and see what happens- the human race is currently playing around with this and other phenomena in the large hadron collider, and might very well unleash forces we scarcely comprehend- not lasting change, but rather we may in time be able to very briefly manifest other realities here. For those who say this is impossible, you will, I believe, in time, join the ranks of those who claimed it was impossible to reach the moon, or to explore the arctic, or that there was "no land mass West of Europe."

One major problem we have is that we regard ourselves as being corporeal and solid because we are capable of sensing other physical objects. It's actually rather strange that we have a stable form since the atoms composing us are primarily empty space- the interactions between these mostly empty particles are still not entirely understood and science continues to search for proof of some other, smaller particle that imparts mass- the higgs-boson, which they claimed to have found, although this is under debate as we speak.

OCCULT PHILOSOPHY

Until fairly recently we didn't even comprehend quarks- the fact that the deeper we dig and the more technology we attain to do so, leads us to smaller and smaller particles, as well as further and further into space with telescopes and other arrays, shows me the truly limitless expanse of both- perhaps even the smallest subatomic particles we theorize to exist are themselves composed of even smaller particles, and those of smaller particles, and so forth until we eventually achieve a minutiae so small we are physically incapable of sensing them. This is very much the same as our theories about the cosmos. For many ages, man considered the cosmos to be (comparatively) small, with the solar system out to Jupiter and then some stars which he imagined were actually in close proximity- for a long time he had no reason to even say the planet was round, even though with a telescope and the moon he could have easily guessed it because of the all-so-obvious spherical shape it manifests due to the crescent shape of light moving across the side exposed to Earth.

Here is another progression which we have enjoined; a century and a half ago we first began to use the telegraph and shortly thereafter telephones and primitive radio systems. Within a few decades we had developed television and radio systems that were far more expansive. Fairly soon the televisions were colored, the radio crystal clear, and satellites began pumping us full of radio waves before the internet became widespread. What we consider modern technology will seem primitive to future generations, despite itself being so much higher in function than that which existed even ten years' past.

So to those claiming theoretical physics are unable to be tested, all you must do is wait- there will come a time, perhaps in our own lives, where such is no longer the case. When we begin to test these theories we will launch ourselves into an entirely new epoch. The occult has a role to play here, even if science does not wish to admit it- the occult posited different planes of existence thousands of years ago in the form of things such as Elysium, Tartarus, the abyss, Helheim, Sheol, Eden, and so forth. Most of these tales could, amusingly, be true in some other reality overlapping out very own. Perhaps over time these bands of reality alter, and our ancestors *did* see such strange things.

OCCULT PHILOSOPHY

The rudiments of atomic theory actually date to ancient Greece-Democritus was a man well beyond his time and theorized that if an object were split into smaller and smaller pieces, it would eventually attain a smallest, indivisible form he termed *atomos*. While he was largely unrecognized for his genius in his time, we now realize he was essentially correct, even realizing these particles could interact with one another.

If the ancients, over 2,000 years ago (2,500 in the case of Democritus) were able to comprehend such things, without the aid of a microscope or any modern scientific gear, we have to give them credit for having been far more intelligent than some generally regard them as being; in reality the dark ages along with severe religious moralism were the primary forces holding back our advancement, to the point where a text on chemistry or herbal lore needed to be couched in "by the power of god I have discovered his mighty plan regarding the stones and herbs"- the knowledge there is now considered superstition by secularists who refuse to understand that most of those works were scientific treatises couched in superstitious language specifically to prevent condemnation by the all-powerful clergy which always sought to burn or behead a few heretical sinners.

Truly, even psychotropics generally refer to this concept of vibration. When a psychedelic is ingested, the most easily observed change is that of the chemistry of the body; the balance of chemicals in the brain is altered, and neurons are triggered through the mundane process of stimulation. However, all of the atoms in the cosmos are not particles so much as they are waves, operating on different wavelengths- physics is coming closer and closer to proving this outright; that what we perceive of as solid matter is essentially composed instead of waves. In this way, the ingestion of a psychotropic also affects the mind's vibration- not in the new age sense, in which vibration is thought of as an *external* field of energy, but rather one which permeates the very particles of which the human mind is composed. The things seen under the influence of such things, then, are very much real, and merely disconnected from normally observable reality. They may even be tangible.

OCCULT PHILOSOPHY

Take, for example, the melting of objects while under the influence of psilocybin mushrooms. In my own past, when I used them, the floor around me began to shift, turn to "jelly," and churn like a slow roiling sea of semi-liquid material. Of course, this shift was utterly intangible- these things I was seeing were not physically there and would not have been visible to anyone around me, had there been anyone there. However, I was able to manipulate this colored matrix of material with my hands in quite the literal, physical sense- I could also manipulate other things which I saw in the same manner. I was also aware of the energy around and within my own body- a sort of aura, as it may be termed.

In fact, at such a high dose (for I had obtained *azurescens* caps instead of normal *cubensis* which has roughly one fourth the psilocin) I appear to have broken into another dimension temporarily- this effect is also seen with salvia divinorum, in which it is completely possible to interact with the things which one sees, assuming that your dose is "just right" such that it doesn't knock you out of all consciousness or fail to produce enough of an effect. The manipulation, in its form there, was not able to be explained in terms of merely "seeing things" but rather in terms of seeing beyond the normal reality around us, such that there was overlap with another. Tesla, again, seems to have understood this; for he remarked that people ought to think of the world in terms of vibration, and considered his brain to be a conduit for cosmic intelligence in some form or another. Even the concept of telepathy is explained here. If it is possible for a vibration or energy to be transmitted through the air from place to place using electrical coils, it should also be possible for two brains to exchange information, if they are able to tune themselves correctly so that the two minds become linked. Various yogis and "psychics" have attempted this with limited if any success, because they have ignored or misunderstood the scientific principle behind the concept itself; it requires a *physical* tuning, not just a mental or spiritual one. Likewise, it wouldn't be possible to use such a power without a spiritual basis to understand it, because science persists in regarding the physical reality around us as the only reality to regard, and the mainstream still rejects theoretical physics, in some cases, as being drug-laden hypothesis alone.

OCCULT PHILOSOPHY

In such a manner we can quantify several occult and psychic phenomena in terms of the manipulation of vibration, wavelength, and so forth.

Telepathy would thus be a connection between two sentient brains through the internal manipulation of the vibration therein, with or without a physical component.

Telekinesis would thus be a connection between one or more sentient brains and a physical object, manipulating its position through the same methods.

Ritualism in the ceremonial sense would thus be the manipulation of reality through steps and rituals designed to alter the former in some way, often through the use of sound, although geometric forms and natural ones are often employed.

Sexual magick is of specific importance in regards to this- when two individuals orgasm simultaneously a great deal of mental energy is quickly released, and subsequently the brains involved quiet down and lose some of their fervor for a time; the perfect setup for a potent ritual. It thus manipulates reality as well, if performed properly.

In all cases it is entirely possible that other realities which interchange with our own are manipulated from both sides on a regular basis, with those doing the manipulating being mostly unawares that they are doing so. We might regard this physical, observable realm and those close to it in wavelength to be similar to chromosomes- within meiosis there is of course the crossing over of genetic material when gametes are formed, and in the same way multiple realities may slowly interchange information and content with one another, *even if most often the change is not observable in the direct sense.*

OCCULT PHILOSOPHY

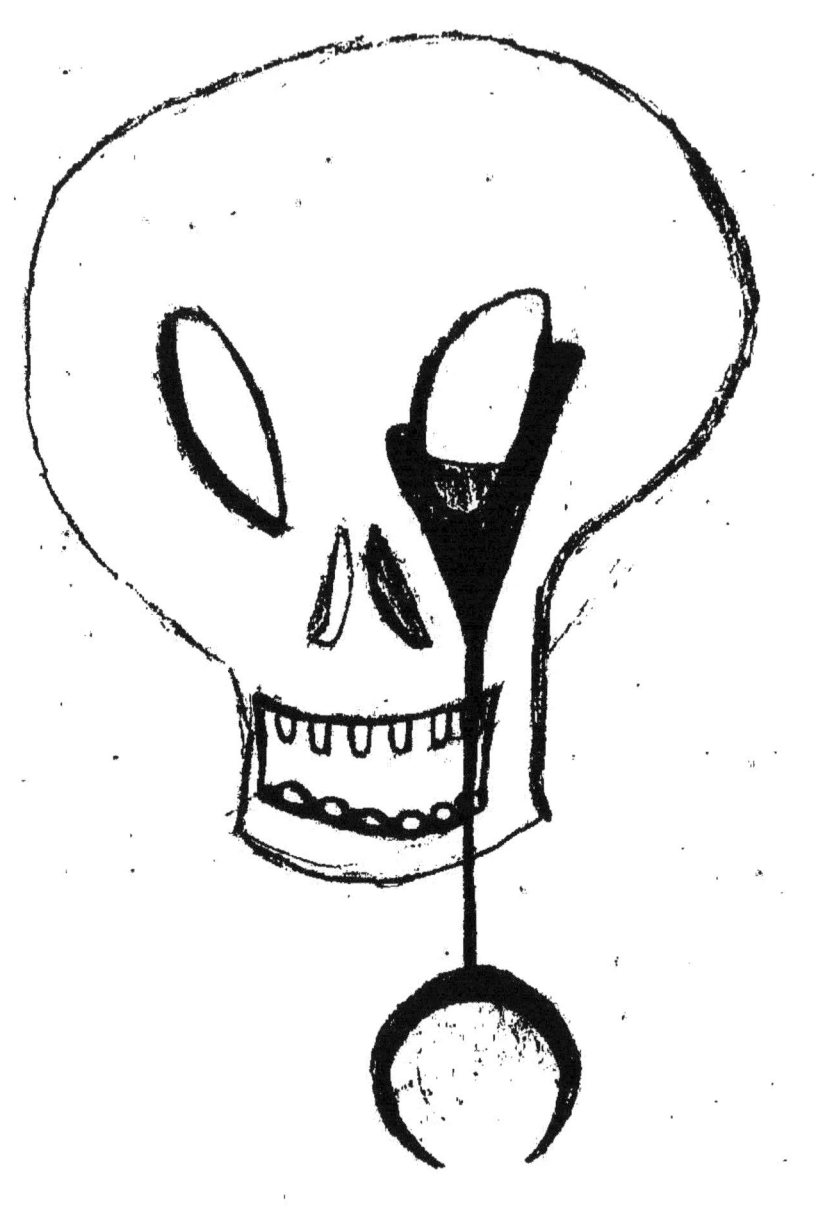

OCCULT PHILOSOPHY

BEYOND THE VEIL OF DEATH

I here must express my own experience with death- my own passing beyond the veil, before I can speak of the topic itself; death is complicated, and it comprises several different phenomena; we speak of death but we must differentiate between biological death, the death of the consciousness, and the transmutation of death.

Years ago, as I was researching psychedelics, I obtained a potent substance- a white powder, a research chemical, largely untested and dangerously toxic. At the time I had already used most of the psychotropics known to man, save for those which were so addictive as to be not worth the time to regard, such as cocaine or heroin. I then proceeded to ingest a dose of this same powder (smoked, not snorted) which very likely would have resulted in death in most users- there had already been others who had suffered brain damage or had a stroke using it, not because of its chemical toxicity so much as its ability to induce stress such that the body would come unbalanced, the heart stopping or something of that ilk.

The resulting experience lasted for days and resulted in a complete overdose followed by months of post traumatic stress that after a year or so finally waned away as I used my mind to heal itself; I merely applied philosophy to my own experience, and spoke with myself internally, slowly undoing the damage done, and drawing something positive from the entire event.

Under this substances' power, the first death was that of biological death- not so much that I had actually died, but that I became convinced I had died. In the sense of death, it may not matter whether it has literally occurred, since the mental change resulting from being convinced one has died is roughly similar- we see the same with certain Haitian rituals, in which a person is poisoned, and put into an unconscious state, after which lasting effects reduce their own sentience to near zero, sometimes for years at a time, but often for shorter periods, depending on the person's ability to resist the psychological after-effects.

OCCULT PHILOSOPHY

I fell out of all consciousness until I felt I was being compressed into an infinitely small point in space- I could sense, in this condition, vibrating waves of light and darkness, which at first spun through my physical form very quickly, like the spinning of a roulette wheel- the roulette of death, so to speak. This cycling of light and dark slowed down over what to me felt like years; for time had slowed to a crawl.

In its final, painstakingly slow cycle, it finally settled on the light. Convinced I had died, I became temporarily aware of my surroundings but was not in control of my body or mind; I heard my own inner voice tell me I had killed my consciousness, and I fought against this, of course, because the experience of biological death is terrifying even for those who have lived a stellar life or died in their sleep- this is self evident, for there is hardly a tale in which a person, once dead, has a happy experience with it until after the biological part is done- with the exception of those who have "died" under the influence of anesthesia or painkillers which deaden the entire experience as their mind slows down.

Thus is the physical stage of death- whether literal or mentally derived. It is a horrifying experience, but one which, after a long period (which to anyone external to it would last at most a few minutes) settles itself on relaxation, once the person becomes aware that they are no longer in the land of the living. I do not claim to know whether my own experience is indicative that all have the same experience, as to finally finding themselves enveloped in light. I also don't claim this has anything to do with Jesus, or a god- for the only external beings I saw were purely demonic, as I will explain.

Following the recognition of death, the mind must then wander through death as well. This experience, for me, had no tinge of terror and was liberating. As I was being carted away to the hospital I again became aware of my surroundings, while being entirely sedated and thus technically incapable of seeing any of the things physically around me. My mind felt opened, and I was able to observe the ambulance in which I was laying.

OCCULT PHILOSOPHY

It was then that I saw it- the land of death itself. It was a phantasmagorical place, full of ash and fire- a Christian would surely have regarded it as Hell, especially since the attending medic slowly came unstuck in the physical world, allowing me to see his aura, and his spirit- in this form, he became quite demonic, his visage transmogrifying into that of a beast, withered with pale flesh, inhaling and exhaling a noxious vapor which to me appeared reddish in color.

At this point any bible believing abrahamist would have begged for forgiveness, but somehow I was entirely unconcerned and unafraid- I made a remark, in my mind, asking whether I was in Hell, and this demonic figure answered, that he thought I didn't believe in such things. As I gazed to my side, the entire wall of the ambulance became transparent, and beyond I could see a great city of the dead- ruined buildings emitting a sort of dusty, fiery vapor as they endlessly dissolved into the blackened skies above. As before I was entirely unconcerned. Others present when I fell out of all consciousness said I was babbling for the most part, and largely unresponsive, but none of them were ever aware that I could easily see things around myself through my mind.

Prior to this I had briefly realized that if I was dead, I was free and no longer had to care about moral strictures or pain (because of course my physical body, I assumed, was already dead and growing cold.) This liberating thought prevented all fear, even if my physical body was still technically alive and in extreme pain- which it was, as I was vomiting uncontrollably and wincing with every movement.

Thus, my mind moved beyond the veil of the physical and into a spiritual realm entirely, in which despite my suffering, my mind had become utterly disconnected from the pain. I was aware of things, but largely unconcerned with them all, and thought little about them.

OCCULT PHILOSOPHY

The sort of strange dissolving and ash and smoke that I saw while utterly beyond consciousness here was a much more powerful but ultimately somewhat similar experience to that of salvia divinorum and in some ways to psilocybin- this is why those substances I regard as particularly important. Many have reported some degree of ego death using both.

Thus even the ego is capable of dying. In this state there is no longer any voluntary, conscious control of the body, and the ego and mind have uncoupled from the former. In this state, one is technically between life and death- their body is still alive, strictly speaking, but the rest of the self is no longer connected to it. The dose I took was so powerful that the next morning I was still utterly dazed and ended up spending some days in the hospital recovering, not because the original experience had terrified me, but rather because the days thereafter were filled with mental confusion and a general lack of energy to do anything other than sleep- at times I acted in a more or less involuntary nature, frequently forgetting things I had only just got through with, such as drinking water. Nonetheless, I recovered completely and at this time have felt perfectly normal for years.

The true terror of the experience was the very first stage of it- the feeling of having died. At first, my mind had run through thinking about how others would react to my succumbing to death, and then thinking about work left undone. After this, though, having come uncoupled from my body, I was no longer concerned with such things. I had been temporarily liberated, and the experience has informed much of my philosophical thought and occult practice since this time. I have given up using all psychotropics since then- firstly, because they no longer appeal to me in any way, and secondly because having already brushed that close to very real death, I felt it would not be appropriate to do so again and perhaps this time biologically succumb- this, because it would hamper my work, which is to release such thoughts to the world. I also realized, that since death is not the end of anything, and I don't need to fear it, that the ultimate good is to enjoy my life while it lasts, and after this to transmute to some other form.

OCCULT PHILOSOPHY

Death is not the end of anything, in reality it is merely a process- part of the never-ending cycle. The divine truth.

When we regard our consciousness, we observe that before we were alive, before we were both born and became aware of our surroundings, we were as nothing- or at least this is how it seems. Unless we accept a few (somewhat dubious) cases where people can "remember their past life" we have to presume that one of two things is true; either our consciousness "began" through some process, or else that we existed before but, as mortals, the biological mind containing our memories is periodically destroyed and our consciousness, the essence of *self,* is transmuted and recycled.

The latter is normally considered wrong or at least dubious by science- this however is gaining popularity, specifically because the concept that the universe did not begin but always existed in some form has also gained momentum. When we regard the physical laws we presume to be true, such as the conservation of mass, we have to give a lot of leeway to a theory such as the big bang because it appears to violate those same laws- or else perhaps some other force is at work, which the religious term "god" but which might as well be any other theoretical, as-yet not understood cosmic force. Rather, it is more sensible to say that this specific dimension, by which I mean the expanse of length, width, and depth which we perceive, has always existed, regardless of whether what we call "the" universe has always existed or not.

Similarly, the process of death is regarded in the same way. We tend to regard ourselves as having been created by biology or divinity at birth, only to exist for a short time as a life form, after which we die- the secularist believes the consciousness thus terminates on both ends- it has a definitive beginning and ending. The religious regard it as terminating at the beginning, with an infinite line extending off endlessly, thus saying that we were created in the beginning but never end.

OCCULT PHILOSOPHY

I have heard few regard it as an endless line in both directions- each individual life-span is merely one cycle, which coils around and terminates, only to spiral off in some other direction, doing so forever. In this manner, any former life is forgotten, but there will be yet more lives after this one, and there were many before. I do not limit this as the easterners do, to life forms on this one planet, but rather believe that life exists elsewhere and thus it is possible for a human to die, only to reincarnate into a form they would currently see as alien.

The ultimate answer to all of these things is simply *infinity*. If there is existence, it is infinite in span, and contains an infinite amount of life. Likewise, if life exists, it exists infinitely- always did and always will, with existence merely vibrating and exchanging information between "strings" of time in higher dimensions. The big bang, thus, if real, was no singular event, but one of a large number of similar events, possibly triggered by the radioactive decay (of a sort) of some particle on a higher dimension which contains, to us, an infinite amount of energy and mass, and in which its own subatomic structure, upon the reaction, exploded into a lower energy level, here becoming seemingly finite though still to our eyes extraordinarily expansive. Our entire universe may be nothing more than an exploded fourth dimensional atom.

In time I believe that mainstream science will embrace such things- it will likely take a great deal of research especially related to physics and astronomy, but in time the notion that the universe is singular, or had a concrete beginning, or is fated to eventually decay away to nothingness until even atoms themselves experience heat death and turn into an undifferentiated soup of subatomic mass will be seen as ridiculous. We might even speak of panspermia- the notion that life on this planet came from some other source, likely extra terrestrial, regardless of whether it was directed or not; this model of life is sensible, although not necessary to explain life. We might fuse this with abiogenesis and say that life here has been affected by outside sources, just as death relates to outside forces beyond our current level of comprehension.

OCCULT PHILOSOPHY

Most of the world fears death- those that don't tend to regard it either as the utter grand finale before being swallowed and consumed by blackness, or else the gate into some eternal realm of paradise or perdition. I have spoken with such people, and remarked that their version of paradise seems like suffering to me, as it is static and largely unchanging- in essence, quite boring. What could be worse, than to spend the rest of eternity in a finite space, with finite things to do? Rather, reincarnation is preferable because the being will never get bored, and always experience things anew, for eternity.

Life and death cannot exist without one another- life slowly grows degraded over time and becomes decrepit- only when it is exhausted and dies does its biological matter get taken up into more fit life forms of a younger age and greater health, and only then can the consciousness also be renewed; the mind is a tool, but it is also a sensory prison, allowing us only to observe a finite space around us. Some believe the ego, upon death, spends a finite amount of time in some other realm; this is possible, although it's also feasible that it reincarnates quite quickly- in either case it matters little because the ultimate effect is the same- the life form loses its memories and experiences a new life. We can, though, take some comfort in this (if we regard this process as having some downfalls)- for life will only be likely to arise under conditions which favor it- a superheated and dusty planet with little atmosphere is unlikely to contain life, at least for any length of time; life is out there, most likely in areas which are fairly similar to Earth, perhaps some being far more easy and gentle an experience than our own planet.

Just as divergent life forms compete to purify one another, so too does death compete with life and degrade it in order to eventually liberate it from its current, aging form, such that it can adopt one which is newer and more healthy. Only through the removal of degraded life forms and detritus can health remain- we see this frequently in fire prone areas, where old growth is largely disheveled, only to be scorched, destroyed, and for new life to spring up under the carbonized branches, fertilized by the ash and cinder from formerly living trees around them.

OCCULT PHILOSOPHY

In fact though this one dichotomy, while sensible in explaining death and its meaning, is also just as useless as any other artificially constructed dichotomy; life and death are merely part of the same cycle of existence, and are not separate except in how we describe and perceive of them. If a thing is alive, and dies, it is still there- only the body has decayed and succumbed.

As long as it holds sentience it will not be destroyed in that sentience- if you burn a piece of wood, it will turn to ashes, and the ashes appear to have lost much of the original mass; this delusion does not account for the release of gas from it as it burns- substances we do not easily perceive without technology, but which are nonetheless present. We only *perceive* the loss of the body, or of the ego. The body is recycled into other life forms, even if embalmed or mummified, and the ego is not lost but transforms and enters a new form which does not remember its past life, thus removing any evidence of the cycle itself.

I do not proclaim reincarnation and the illusion of life and death as separate, based on some vague spiritual "beliefs" which I hold- I proclaim them as evident based on established physical laws, just as the alchemical processes of old, if properly interpreted, are statements from eminent chemists and biologists of their age, hidden from the laypeople. The occult, though, goes a step further, in attempting not to proclaim the existence of such forces and phenomena, but rather to adequately describe and in some cases attempt to manipulate them.

There is *no* dichotomy which is not artificial. Light and darkness are part of the same form, regarding only more or less photons being present. Hot and cold is an illusion also (which is just the presence or absence of more energy.) Life and death as we understand them are merely opposing, oscillating forces within one cycle- to regard them as entirely separate we might as well posit that protons and electrons aren't part of the same atom, complimenting one another and creating existence itself in atomic form.

OCCULT PHILOSOPHY

CONCLUSION: OCCULT PRINCIPLES

The principles of the occult which concern this work are essentially simple- there are many conclusions to draw from them, and many issues which they connect to, but the concepts themselves are exceptionally easy to understand. This is yet another similarity; in this case between the philosophy itself and the spiritual realm, for the spiritual is far-reaching and complicated, but when looked at from a proper angle it becomes easier to work with. The principles are several; infinite nature, cyclical nature, and purification.

First and foremost, and by far the most important of all principles here is simply that of infinite nature; things persist once they have arisen, and would have existed prior to arising in their current form. The fact that we are not aware of our past, beyond our current form, is largely meaningless, because our conception of having existed only for a finite period of time is prefaced by our inability to remember former lives. Nonetheless, physics itself posits a conservation of all things, and it is difficult to understand why we ought to separate preservation of the consciousness (or soul) from preservation of any other extant thing or force. From this principle we garner reincarnation itself; for it is the only means by which this and the next principle can be identified in a system in which life forms on a biological basis come and go, living only to eventually die and decay.

The second principle is that of the cycle, for that is what everything undergoes within our physical realm- such as it is as well on the spiritual plane, for the two are not entirely separate. Culture, biology, spiritual systems, and everything else, undergo cycles over time, often complicated ones which connect to one another like gears in a gigantic machine of life. In this way, we can derived that arts such as divination are possible, but difficult, and that a great deal of observation is necessary to adequately predict outcomes. This mathematical principle applies also to oscillation, which is little more than a cycle involving two paired aspects, such as light and dark.

OCCULT PHILOSOPHY

The third principle is that of purification, for this is an ongoing process and directly pairs with biological evolution as well as other forms of selection. A life form on Earth is not unlike any other life form on Earth- they are all divergent forms of the same one life source. As such, these diverged forms compete, and thus improve one another within the context of the current climate, environment, and availability of energy resources. Likewise, spiritual systems and cultures do the same, and cultures and their beliefs compete on the exact same basis, also purifying themselves over time in response to stimuli. Here we must be careful not to conflate temporary improvement with permanent improvement- the latter does not exist in a dynamic system prone to drastic change either slow or sudden.

When the occultist delves into such things, their mind is greatly improved. It is *not possible* to truly practice magick in any of its many forms without the capability of critical thinking, and those without a curious nature may find themselves self limiting by ingesting only work from one specific occult school.

We then reach the final conclusion; much of what we see is an illusion, as some before have pointed out, but few have corresponded to such other principles. Life and death are just opposite sides of the same single coin, as are good and evil, and the cosmos, slowly whirling around in time, could be utterly destroyed as science suggests, at some future point, through collision or heat death, and the ultimate effect on our own existence would be scarcely felt, for the cosmos is still there in another dimension. In particular, this principle is important; the existence of other dimensions can adequately explain (at least in spiritual terms) all manner of manifestations and visions.

It suffices to say simply this; that there is no destruction at all, simply because creation and destruction are merely flip sides of the same ongoing cycle, and in reality are technically illusions.

OCCULT PHILOSOPHY

Printed in Poland
by Amazon Fulfillment
Poland Sp. z o.o., Wrocław